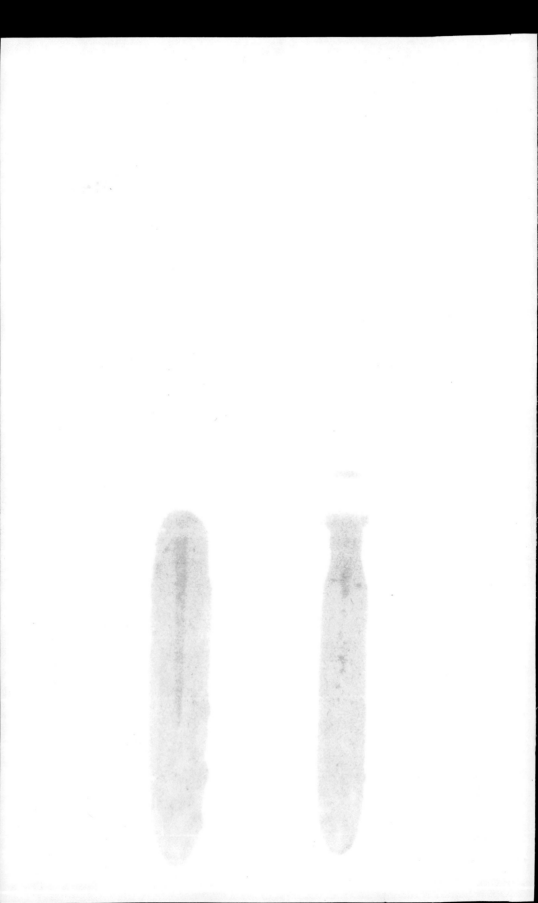

*Manuscript Solicitation
for Libraries, Special Collections,
Museums, and Archives*

Manuscript Solicitation
for
Libraries, Special Collections, Museums, and Archives

Edward C. Kemp
Acquisition-Special Collections Librarian
University of Oregon

1978

Libraries Unlimited, Inc.
Littleton, Colo.

LIBRARIES UNLIMITED, INC.
P.O. Box 263
Littleton, Colorado 80160

Library of Congress Cataloging in Publication Data

Kemp, Edward C., 1929-
    Manuscript solicitation for libraries, special
collections, museums, and archives.

    Bibliography: p.194
    Includes indexes.
    1. Acquisition of manuscripts. 2. Libraries
--Gifts, legacies. I. Title.
Z689.K45   025.2'1   77-29015
ISBN 0-87287-183-5

TABLE OF CONTENTS

Introduction   7

Chapter 1—PLANNING A SOLICITATION PROGRAM   11

Chapter 2—POTENTIAL COLLECTION SPECIALTIES   18

Chapter 3—MATERIALS TO SOLICIT   24

Chapter 4—SOURCES OF DONATIONS—LEADS   33

Chapter 5—CORRESPONDENCE   43

Chapter 6—VISITING THE DONOR   48

Chapter 7—RECEIPT, SORTING, ORGANIZATION, DESCRIPTION,
           AND FINANCIAL APPRAISAL   58

Chapter 8—MAINTAINING DONOR INTEREST   68

Chapter 9—ILLUSTRATORS AND AUTHORS OF BOOKS FOR
           CHILDREN: A Study of Collecting on a National
           Basis   76

Chapter 10—THE MUNICIPAL MUSIC COLLECTION: A Working
            Example of a Larger Municipal Library's
            Solicitation Program   89

Chapter 11—THE BOOK GIFT 105

Chapter 12—PROFESSIONAL AND PERSONAL QUALITIES 116

Chapter 13—BENEFITS GAINED FROM A SOLICITATION
PROGRAM 123

List of Appendices 127

Bibliography 194

Subject Index 203

INTRODUCTION

Few explanations of how to build a library or historical society manuscript collection appear in professional literature. More diverting are the publications by Lawrence Clark Powell, Lawrence Thompson, and David Randall on the pleasure of collecting and the treasures acquired. This book presents a practical approach to a collecting program without expenditure for acquisition, but with the usual overhead for staff, supplies, and incidentals. Few libraries have funds for all necessary purchases, and active solicitation of gift materials seems especially appropriate. The same thoughts, advice, and techniques are as applicable to the large or small historical museum as to the public, college, special, or university library.

Many institutions depend upon divine predestination for gifts. The library waits for the donation to be delivered unto its door, because a potential donor lives within the community, is an alumnus, or is reportedly planning to bequeath his materials to the institution. Such reasoning often defies belief when examined carefully, and all such library aspirations ought to be reexamined objectively. "Predestined" gifts are probably so arranged only in the mind of the librarian, and meanwhile may be lost to fire, flood, silverfish, relatives, or to fragmentation through sale or gifts to friends, admirers, and associates. For every potential gift collection which remains intact, many more are lost. Our library has rescued a congressman's files from an outdoor trash burner, has lost a significant diary to a bathtub where the potential donor took the volume for one last reading, has spared good historical corporate records from twelve trash cans, and has removed roach powder from forty cartons of political correspondence. Today's scholar rarely gathers and maintains his own research files but relies on the special collections of a good library to provide unusually deep, rich source materials.

As book and manuscript collecting have become institutional rather than private, the basis for collecting has widened. Interest in manuscripts is no longer restricted to papers of presidents, successful politicians, and established literary figures. Researchers and collectors have discovered the importance of secondary figures, "also-rans," and articulate citizens. Today's librarians seek manuscript or printed records of minority groups. These sources, ignored by past generations of collectors, add to our knowledge of what we are and how we came to be what we are.

When such materials are not lost or dispersed, but rescued and preserved in an appropriate library, they enrich the institution, changing its quality and focusing upon a new potential, bringing a fresh contribution to history and scholarship, as well as providing verification or refutation of earlier research. The gift may represent a collection of letters, diaries, journals, speeches, pamphlets, manuscripts, or books, or all of these, assembled or created as an intelligent unit. The collection has been brought together over a period of years with knowledge, funds, talent, zeal, and patience that few librarians can afford to devote to one specialty.

The librarian must assess such collections to make certain of their usefulness to the institution. The collector in his passion may assemble or even invent items that really do not belong within the scope of the collection. We recall one splendid collection of Lincolniana which included autographs, books, letters, offprints and tearsheets, articles, newspapers, and a jar of soil on which Lincoln had trod. Another potential donor produced both journals and letters written by white men in the Northwest long before any had set foot in the region. Eventually, the donor brought forth authentic materials, and whether he did this because we had passed his history examination or simply because we did not accept the fraudulent materials, we never learned. The collection, too, may display the collector's ignorance or blind spots and may contain secondary items of no special interest to the library.

The writer has had twenty years experience in seeking major gifts for the University of Oregon Library. While the program was initially based on special collections within the state of Oregon, it grew quickly to encompass the Northwest and rather logically to emphasize nationally significant gifts in specialized subject areas. The diverse collecting interests reflect the use and support given by academic departments, as well as the professional judgment of several librarians. In the twenty years of active collecting, the library has received $3,500,000 in terms of manuscripts, journals, original illustrations and art, books, sheet music, and similar donations.

Colleges and universities can use such solicitation to support both the undergraduate and graduate programs, to encourage research on campus, to attract special students and faculty, to support accreditation, and to enhance the prestige of the school. The public library may have an obligation to its community to collect and preserve local material and regional records or may seek to support existing strength through active solicitation; the benefits which accrue are similar to those of the academic library. While solicitation enriches the librarian's knowledge of community, the community in turn learns about the library, its activities, and its needs. A stronger library, an interested community, and more financial support from the parent body may logically result.

The local, county, or state museum has generally accepted those gifts offered to it, but seldom has it taken an active role in seeking out specific collections. More often it may issue a catch-all, mimeographed letter to the heirs of a recently deceased community member, appealing for letters, typewriters, wagon wheels, books, and kitchen implements. While this appeal does satisfy an obligation to collect and preserve for its public, the museum ought to use more appropriate means of soliciting what it sincerely needs. With better regional collections, the museum encourages use, enjoyment, and research, and enhances its reputation in terms of materials and support.

Potential donors exist within every community, from the family of readers which needs space for new books, to the family which never read but which retained all its ancestor's letters in the attic. Library users are often unaware of the library's needs and special interests. It takes little time to strike up a conversation, with some salient comments on the library's desires for special materials, often based upon what the reader has borrowed. In reviewing old library files concerning previous gifts, the librarian can renew the relationships already established to see whether further material exists and/or whether the donor favors the library. Satisfied donors create additional gifts, either from their own homes or offices or through their associations with others. Upon embarking on a program, the new librarian might well consider talking with unhappy donors to learn what went wrong; perhaps making amends may evoke the formerly proffered gift or a new gift.

The most devoted library supporters may exist among the library staff; have they ever been asked for contributions or suggestions of possible donors? The input from library employees provides new opportunities, as does work among community organizations. Those silent sources on the library shelves—bibliographies, city directories, telephone books, biographical dictionaries, professional directories—offer an almost limitless supply of possible donors.

With the name of a potential donor in hand, proper preparation for solicitation is vital. The librarian must know something about the field, the individual, and his accomplishments and situation. Only then is contact in order. An introductory letter, rather than a telephone call or personal visit, is more satisfactory. A letter identifies the institution and its writer, the general program and interest which provoked the letter, and, most important, the reason the librarian has written the recipient. While large institutions often use form letters and half a dozen letterheads adapted to the type of material sought, a more sincere, direct, personal approach is advised. Many potential donors, while flattered to have interest displayed in their work, easily recognize a form letter which displays a blank or two with the prospective donor's name and occupation. If the collection is good, he may well have received several such letters, and he doubts the sincerity of librarians. The prospective donor today has too many unsolicited letters, telephone calls, or door-to-door salesmen to put much credence in a form letter. A well-written, personal letter establishes the tone of future negotiations.

Receiving a response by mail or telephone is the librarian's initial reward from the prospective donor: he has said something. If the answer indicates any interest at all, it is important to act quickly: write, telephone, or visit. A gift is possible and a delayed response may confirm the donor's doubts: did they really mean me, do they really want my collection, are they as dilatory as I have heard? Immediate response may be simply a promise of a future meeting.

Meeting the potential donor allows each party to establish certain things about the other. The donor may have further questions; the librarian is anxious to see and assess the material's value to the library. That meeting, unless preceded by correspondence, must establish all those matters which normally occur by mail, and it is very easy to forget all the details when viewing an exciting collection. Any new facts developed by either party ought to be reconfirmed when the librarian writes the prospective donor further. The librarian may well personify the institution in the donor's eyes, and his performance should be based on this role.

The initial visit may actually produce a good gift, or a token, or the major gift, or it may lead to further visits and courtship of the donor. The librarian's written records—notes, correspondence, and perhaps a work diary—become vital to final acquisition of the entire gift. Maintaining the donor's interest, his support, his friendship produces further benefits which add to the library's collection or to its financial support.

Little true exchange of information exists on techniques among librarians who seek donations, for the field is competitive. This text is written for the librarian with imagination and vision who can develop his own program after consideration of the suggestions contained herein.

Special appreciation is owed to H. William Axford, who suggested the subject as a book, and to Martin Schmitt, who, with Eugene Barnes, conceived the bases of the university library solicitation program at Oregon, and who has travelled far and wide with me in the pursuit of gifts, good and bad. My wife has worked with me in the library and in field situations, no matter what the circumstances, and she has never failed to provide the proper dinner and library-oriented evening for the unexpected, drop-in library donor: Elaine deserves all my appreciation for a successful program.

E.C.K.

Chapter 1

PLANNING A SOLICITATION PROGRAM

KNOWLEDGE OF THE LIBRARY RESOURCES

In conceiving a library or museum solicitation program, the librarian, archivist, or curator must take time to become familiar with his institution, to know and appreciate its needs, strengths, weaknesses, size, directions, staffing, and goals; to examine the present user community and to envision the potential depth and scope of future use; to assess available resources in funds, staff, and building; and to ascertain present and potential support from the board, staff, and community.

Librarians, museum curators, and archivists utilize similar collection-building techniques. Therefore, to spare the reader verbiage, the planning, soliciting, collecting individual representing an institution is called a "librarian" and given the old-fashioned textual pronoun "he."

The librarian must recognize his library's strengths in which he can take pride when talking with potential donors. More important, he must be aware of fields which are especially weak, and know specifically what types of materials, such as reference volumes, academic press books, journals, general surveys, or introductory texts are needed. For example, with severe budgetary problems in the early and mid-1930s, the University of Oregon Library (from which most examples in this text will be drawn) curtailed its purchase of university press books, and any serious use of the collection would once have shown this gap. Until the early 1950s, a business administration professor collected railroad history, but with his departure, the collection paralleled the plight of the American railways: it lagged behind without funds, leadership, acquisition of new material, replacement of outmoded equipment, and, most important, users. The librarian must recognize such situations and seize upon the proper occasion to remedy them.

EVALUATION OF TYPE OF LIBRARY AND ITS USERS

Each type of library has its special collection, scope, and users. The user of a small public library does not seek primary resource materials (manuscripts, such as journals, diaries, letters, speeches, or handwritten reports) but probably would welcome a collection of good recent books in his subject area. Those books might be the goal of a local solicitation effort: which townspeople might own the books and willingly donate them to the library? The metropolitan library might be expected to have primary source materials, such as first-hand accounts (minute books, financial reports, and correspondence) of local clubs or associations which were active over a long period of years. If the city has an historical society or museum, the records could be located there. If the records are not in public hands, a local solicitation program to seek them from associations or long-term members is in order. The junior college with several specialties might gather appropriate professional or vocational journals if the library is not microfilm-oriented. It might solicit the district newspaper's files and morgue to support an on-going history program.

The librarian must recognize the type of library he represents. He knows his book, serial, pamphlet, and journal collection as well as its scope, inadequacies, and currency; he is aware of manuscript holdings; he knows what use his patrons make of existing collections; and he anticipates some potential projects based on the collection. As its field representative, he is a walking catalog of the library. If he lacks the answer to a donor's question, he secures and supplies the response, not only to satisfy the donor, but to add to his own knowledge.

The local or city library will rarely begin a manuscripts solicitation program at the national level, realizing that solicitation, shipment, examination, arrangement, evaluation, maintenance, and service require staff, space, and supplies. Commitment to a solicitation program extends for an indefinite period and may burden successors with problems of unwanted gifts, staff, space, and budget. It is one thing to discard a copy of a book; another to dispose of a unique manuscript. Pressure upon the local library by one researcher to seek manuscript materials should be evaluated; does a city library have any role in collecting working files of prominent Americans? Should a junior college library attempt to build a literary manuscript collection by soliciting files from all noted science fiction writers? Unless funds, supporting material, physical space, and appropriate users exist, the library's decision should be negative.

Regardless of the size and scope of the library, the librarian must examine the services, holdings, and programs of neighboring institutions. Does his plan to solicit in special fields conflict with other agencies with well-established programs or with a private collection which is well funded?

Does the library have access to adequate finances to undertake a program on a continuing basis? Funds need to be expended for staff, solicitation, organization, and service; to purchase supplies and equipment, such as acid-free folders, stationery, and storage cartons; and to revamp a section of the library into a secure, fire-proof, theft-proof storage area.

STAFFING: FLEXIBILITY IN SIZE AND FUNCTIONS

A program can be correlated to available time and staff. For fifteen or more years, our university library solicitation staff has included one professional librarian, one or two clerical assistants, and four to six student assistants. The section's staff has grown or diminished to meet more immediate demands in other sections of the library. While such an operation can easily snowball with an active staff, it can retrench to a warehouse operation, simply storing received materials. However, the institution is obligated to its users and to donors to organize its collections and make them accessible and available.

While a flexible program might well be desirable in terms of administrative budgeting, the collector-librarian would be far happier with a reliable staffing pattern. A college or university staff might include two professional librarians, one to handle development of leads, solicitation, and travel; the other to supervise the processing and use of materials. Three clerical staff members would prepare solicitation correspondence, maintain files, and do preliminary manuscript organization. A smaller institution might have to depend on a part-time professional and assistant. This text will not address long-term maintenance and service responsibilities. Kenneth Duckett's book, *Modern Manuscripts: A Practical Manual for Their Management, Care, and Use* (Nashville, Tenn.: American Association for State and Local History, 1975) provides necessary details.

SCOPE OF THE SOLICITATION PROGRAM

Given knowledge of the institution, collections, users, and community, the librarian develops general solicitation guidelines. Among the considerations are types of materials, size and scope of the collection, and subject specialties. Such guidelines are essential for, in the enthusiasm of collecting, it is far too easy to accept everything, without consideration of present and future use and commitments.

The library and the librarian set limits and directions; local historical societies occasionally show the result of indiscriminate collecting, reflecting all periods and all parts of the world with souvenir objects displayed among a few fine pieces. While manuscripts can be diverse, the program must have limits. A collection should not be accepted just because it is offered, but only if it is within the library's collecting sphere. One small college in our area refused an offer of the papers of a Supreme Court justice, realizing that it lacked funds and staff to organize and maintain the files, as well as the faculty and students to use the collection well. This was a rare response; more often the librarian finds it easier to accept a gift to avoid a difficult personal or political situation or with a hope that the library may grow in supporting material and users to match the gift. Some gifts may add grace or prestige to a library, but unless they contribute to the library in a significant intellectual manner, it is far better to suggest alternatives, such as other institutions that may provide better facilities and more users. Embarking on a new subject area is expensive, for a manuscript collection is of little use without supporting books, journals, periodicals, and pamphlets already properly cataloged.

To announce immediately that the library will build a national center for a specialized field, be it science fiction, Western outlaw history, conservation, Native American newspapers, or conservative publications, is a major error. Many programs have been launched with publicity and fanfare, only to fall flat. The announcement of grandiose plans generally exhibits an ignorance of what has been and is being collected, and often of the field itself. This type of publicity rarely provokes unsolicited gifts of any merit; on the contrary, donations are generally of marginal value or perhaps not worthy of retention. The librarian ought to solicit actively gifts appropriate to the library rather than to expect a flood of publicity and appeals to attract substantive gifts.

The librarian must be constantly aware of the scope of the library program. Is the collection to include exhibition materials with some local color, such as photographs or posters? Is the library seeking published materials, books that focus upon aspects of the community or state? Does the collection include regional political history—correspondence, speeches, committee reports? Are these materials for use in a local library, a city library, a state library, or a university library? Is the material collected for a local library suitable: does it reflect the community or does it pertain more directly to another region? Should the city library work with writers, foundations, charities, clubs, businesses, and printing concerns in order to secure a wide variety of materials published about or within the city? Should this be a function of the city library, museum, or archives?

Each solicited gift must represent something useful to the library; it ought not to cause embarrassment 25 years later or be neglected as a resource. The gift should be something attainable; it is senseless to solicit in well-established areas which demand a financial premium, such as twentieth-century American literature, Revolutionary War history, or California forty-niners' diaries. These items were not always in demand, and they were once accumulated at little expense. The librarian should collect at the right time, viewing the present and future potential of what is presently available.

DEVELOPMENT OF THE PROGRAM

The library program might start in a small fashion in an area of immediate interest with which the librarian can become familiar. He examines *The National Union Catalog of Manuscript Collections* and Hamer's *Guide to Historical Manuscripts*; reads the special literature unique to the field; talks with those who know the field—its past and present leaders; and determines which other institutions might work or might have worked within the same area. With this knowledge, he considers whether to proceed.

Some years ago our library sought several collections created and maintained by forestry experts. The subject was of regional importance; the collections existed within the Northwest, assembled and created by international authorities. Through correspondence and subsequent visits with these potential donors, the library secured files and diaries, and then expanded its program, finding many business and personal records covering the history and westward movement of the timber industry. By collecting the local records of an individual lumberman, we learned that his family roots were in Minnesota and Wisconsin, and, indeed, earlier family had traveled from New England and the southeastern forests; the logical step was to secure records from all extant family members, and thus to recreate one family's participation in the industry. Conservationists, lumber companies, Forest Service administrators, and wilderness groups donated their files to build, support, diversify, and enrich a collection which had begun with files of several important foresters.

With some support from our music school, the library solicited American sheet music, the kind of music that turned up in every piano bench, in most attics, and occasionally in handsomely bound volumes. Today, a computer index to the entire collection is in preparation.

AWARENESS OF NEW FIELDS

While the librarian focuses his attention on his immediate project, he attempts to discern subjects previously ignored for research purposes. Our library encountered a large group of missionary diaries, letters, sermons, and publications assembled in India during the last century. The material seemed of no special interest to us, for we assumed that the manuscripts contained only religious matters, such as the winning of souls. With a little reflection, we changed our minds and sought the gift. We then gathered intensively in a new field, missionary history, which has been explored within the last six years by three other major libraries as well as denominational headquarters. Until very recently, the mission board libraries emphasized administrative and fiscal records, ignoring personal items. We used a direct approach, seeking materials assembled by those who were trained and educated for their work abroad; who created prime research documents—letters and diaries; and who wrote of their findings for publication on their mission presses. Often these manuscripts and pamphlets contain first-hand accounts of local customs and traditions: a history of porcelain and its manufacture, an understanding of local society and politics, a report on the economic system, a treatise on shop signs or street cries, an appreciation of an art form or music, or the last transcription of a local dialect. While working within established guide lines is important, it is also important to be flexible and open to new fields which add to the library's resources and are supported by the library collection.

INITIATION OF A SMALL PROGRAM
BRINGS PRACTICAL EXPERIENCE AND ADVANTAGES

A simple solicitation program permits the novice to learn much about solicitation per se and the concomitant responsibilities: the need to organize, maintain, arrange, and support the donations. A major publishing house announced that it would organize and store for research purposes the papers of those included in its biographical directories. Can a publisher afford the professional staff to select, discard, and organize historical manuscripts, let alone provide users with the necessary supporting books, journals, and facilities, and then service the collection indefinitely? Premature publicity and commitments beyond institutional capability are ill-advised.

Working locally and quietly, the librarian can make the mistakes which are part of learning—allowing himself too much time with the donor, traveling on a wild goose chase, committing social *faux pas*, or accepting an unwanted gift in order to escape an uncomfortable situation. He learns to cope with an overbearing donor who has only a few tokens and demands too much time and attention; he establishes community support as he explores those attics, basements, and even private libraries, to which he can find the proper entrée. He familiarizes himself with a special view of local philanthropy to enrich the collecting program. While working within his community, the librarian educates himself in a broader approach to solicitation, because the same techniques apply regionally or nationally. With local experience, the library may expand its collecting program, provided there are sufficient user interest, financial resources, and supporting collections.

Chapter 2

POTENTIAL COLLECTION SPECIALTIES

Collecting fields are as diverse as the library's needs and the librarian's imagination, but they should focus upon a period, event, personage, subject area, or several common matters. In initiating a solicitation program with a small scope or base from which to test and learn, the librarian might consider seeking local history, which will enrich the library regardless of its size. Certain types of collections transcend the supposed levels of sophistication among libraries.

For example, a library with an interest in music has wide possibilities for increasing its resources. Individual musicians, composers, performers, and managers may all possess manuscripts, scores, correspondence, books, music, posters, arrangements, tapes, or recordings. Musical groups, whether civic-sponsored, chamber, symphonic, or popular, have recordings or tapes, programs, press releases, reviews, posters, correspondence, and music in all forms. The folk singer may have transcriptions for the small library concerned with local materials or for the large library interested in local folk music and culture.

LOCAL CULTURAL AND SOCIAL HISTORY

In most communities, civic improvement clubs have existed for many years. These usually include music associations, small orchestral groups, theater companies, reading or literary societies, discussion clubs, debating leagues, and similar organizations with common bonds. The librarian should discover whether these associations maintained the treasurer's books, secretary's minutes, president's correspondence, and associated records. Were civic groups formed to promote passage of specific local legislation? Where are those records? What brochures, pamphlets, or local magazines have been published to chronicle or support some aspect of the community?

To take one example, has the local theater group kept records? It, or one of its long-time leaders, might well have not only the usual scrapbooks of press clippings and glossy photographs of the performers, but it may have retained programs, posters, scripts, plays written locally for specific celebrations, or musical scores. When organized and inventoried, could this same material support a study of the group, of drama within the town or region, of contemporary life, or even a successful re-creation of a play years after the original production. Would such files help the present group, contribute to a national history, or benefit the drama student?

LOCAL ENVIRONMENTAL HISTORY

With contemporary emphasis on the environment, the serious student seeks older records of local flora and fauna. Where would these records exist?

This subject area, not often explored by the collecting librarian, contains a wealth of material. By reading newspaper files and local publications, the librarian identifies amateur naturalists who may possess letters and diaries, field notes, sighting lists, photographs, and similar records. Many communities have one or more long-established natural history groups, devoted to birding, hiking, geological expeditions, and even to conservation. To know what birds were observed twenty-five, fifty, or one hundred years ago is a fascinating subject for layman and ornithologist alike.

While examining the subject area, the librarian would also locate writers of local pamphlets or contributors to national or regional magazines. Do these local natural history writers have unpublished materials? Do they have unpublished personal records or accounts from other naturalists? Often the researcher instinctively or intuitively gathered personal materials from others but did not use the data. Did anyone within the community specialize, either professionally or as an amateur, in wildlife photography? The working records of the professor whose avocational interests deal with some aspect of local nature lore are collectible. Even the town recluse or hermit may well have kept an account of his life within his natural environment—the local Thoreau.

LOCAL PROFESSIONAL HISTORY

While an attorney's files may be considered confidential, especially within a small community, some aspects of his work are publicly and historically significant. Is the attorney willing to donate his files concerning the struggle to protect or vacate or convert a former military base, to create a wildlife refuge or to seek its abandonment, to introduce or prevent immigrant or cheap labor, to establish a new community industry, to support an issue or candidate? One of our most interesting attorneys wished to be known as a "defender of women and children," which his files amply support. A small library may not wish to consider medical files, but a large institution with a medical school may seek the records of a long-established doctor. Few such collections remain in the Northwest, simply because no thought was given to reviewing records for selective preservation as succeeding generations faced the problem of how to handle old files.

Proceedings of professional associations, published or not, present an historical account of the profession within the region. While the local minister serves the community as religious leader, his records have a further value. Were his sermons topical and concerned with problems of the community seventy-five years ago? Was he unusually perceptive or articulate? Did he summarize in sermon notes or record in manuscript or published sermons or speeches before civic groups his observations about the community? The minister's record books, listing marriages, births, and deaths, have a local historical value. His professional library is a reflection of contemporary philosophers and theologians.

LOCAL BUSINESS HISTORY

Have local businesses flourished within the community, and is their history intertwined with that of the community? Did some assume major roles in war-time or with the ascendency of a trend or fad? Our library received the records of one Western saddle-maker, in business for over one hundred years, whose enterprise declined with the arrival of the automobile and ascended only some sixty years later with the arrival on television of the cowboy with chaps, saddle, and holster. Those files included minute books, correspondence, advertising, financial accounts, and the concern's own catalogs. Not only would such a collection be of interest to a local library, but it would be useful to a large library emphasizing business history.

If any cartographic business operated for many years, its files are important to a local, regional, or state library. The engineering or survey company may possess maps and other geographical records, revealing changes in the area. Is there a well-established bookstore which still retains its files? Not only has the library an opportunity to secure a good business account, but selfishly it has the opportunity to examine the records to identify book collectors of years past and to seek out those collectors or their heirs, who might be willing to donate to the library.

By approaching an old, local business, the librarian meets with either administrative staff or older employees, gaining from either support for his program or suggestions of other old firms, owners, and employees. Often the care of correspondence and key records is the responsibility of the senior clerk, retained because of his familiarity with the files. The records have become, by default and his devotion, his personal responsibility, and he will either view the librarian with relief, knowing the librarian will preserve the records permanently, or with suspicion, fearing his job security, or believing that only he could ever comprehend the details of the business accounts. The librarian has either an immediate friend or a long-term job to prove the sincerity of his interest. The chief clerk deserves much praise, for he has spared the records from every new administrative housecleaning and efficiency study.

Business records are often bulky and take considerable space. The librarian needs to consider a large group of business records carefully before acceptance. The library should be free to discard whatever it wishes, as the majority of business files are of daily, routine nature—invoices, cancelled checks, bills, and time cards. The librarian should attempt to keep only the overall, basic records, summarizing activities of the business. One gift from a major business could overwhelm a small library.

The local photographer occasionally assembled or retained a huge collection of old negatives, just as the architect may have vast files of old drawings, renderings, plans, models, specifications, and correspondence. These materials, if properly cared for and well identified, represent treasures to the librarian. Both provide exacting, graphic records of the community, which benefit the local or regional historian, or national researcher.

The photographer and architect may have books and professional journals of special value. In fact, a run of good photographic magazines is a prize, as is the older architectural journal. Old catalogs of materials, supplies, and equipment issued by manufacturers or jobbers reflect the contemporary sources for both vocations.

Banks, real estate offices, and insurance companies may have files of city directories or telephone books which pre-date the library's set. They are important for the librarian's historical research, as is explained later. The various annuals received by a bank or insurance firm are useful and often available as gifts. The contact with each concern leads to further gifts from it or its associates. The Chamber of Commerce may have a directory file, too, along with correspondence and supporting data promoting the community, region, and perhaps special business interests.

LOCAL SOCIAL OR PERSONAL HISTORY

Many towns or cities retain certain archival, formal records, which document local administrative history. Such archives lack local social history as recorded by an articulate citizen. Similarly, academic, institutional archives contain only formal administrative reports and proceedings, lacking informal narrative accounts of students and faculty. The personal record, a form of social history, is rarely spared and saved, except for the benefit of family or through the efforts of the librarian. An individual creates a personal narrative, either in the form of diaries or journals, or through letters written regularly to a good friend or relative. The importance of such fresh, personal, uncalculated records cannot be underestimated. However, the librarian's diligent search for such records is generally the only means of discovery. The librarian must learn who has kept diaries, who wrote descriptive letters with regularity. A formal history needs an informal flavor to make it an entertaining, enjoyable record.

Letters between relatives or friends can be excellent; the writers' interests and comments may range far and wide, yet their positions reflect no special standing within the community.

The social club, whether a sewing circle, church women's group, men's fraternal order, war veterans' association, religious fellowship, or bicycling club may have records. Groups formed to send clothes to destitute people abroad, to support the troops during war-time, to promote or condemn a temperance drive, to advance a local school or governmental issue, may have maintained files, circulated petitions, issued literature, written letters, and prepared posters or broadsides. Through familiarity with his community organizations, the librarian gains a sense of local history and a broader perspective of his community's place in regional and national development.

LOCAL COLLECTING MAY LEAD TO NATIONAL COLLECTIONS

A public or county library or museum may well wish to consider the above suggestions, with application to its own needs. On the other hand, while learning his craft at the local level, the librarian has prepared himself for collecting on a larger scale. Once the librarian has developed his collecting skills, he need not heed local geographical boundaries but can expand his scope to encompass regional or national collections which fit within the subject areas sought by his library.

NATIONAL COLLECTIONS

Given the facilities, sufficient funds, supporting collections, users, and staff to build and maintain a national collection, the librarian should seek national collections if and when they relate to and support the library and institutional program. Our work on a national basis is very selective; collections are solicited from key people within our special areas of interest, after an assessment of their materials.

Present and future use of a collection plays a vital role in the librarian's thinking. Our library's forestry materials, mentioned in the first chapter, attained national prominence with the acquisition of papers collected within our geographical region. To expand such a collection was a reasonable, logical step, and soliciting and attracting papers of other foresters and lumbermen was far easier with a major collection in hand. Other schools and foundations became interested, but our library had already gathered many collections before forest history became a field of national collecting interest.

In the following chapters, we suggest means of locating possible donors on a national basis, but it is up to each library to determine its own directions. To suggest that all libraries collect the files of bankers, actors, politicians, sociologists, writers, physicists, poets, economists, dramatists, engineers, and musicians would be as unwise and wasteful as for each library to concentrate on building a collection of newspaper poets or self-published political or religious theorists.

Each librarian must adapt his solicitation vision to the present needs of the library. Through solicitation, the librarian builds the library and increases his knowledge of special subject areas and his ability to work with all kinds of donors. Recognizing the future needs of the library presents an opportunity to acquire now books and manuscripts at a substantial saving of funds and staff time.

Chapter 3

MATERIALS TO SOLICIT

To collect manuscripts within a given profession, era, or subject interest, the librarian needs to know the special manuscript materials and books common to the field. In other terms, he must be familiar with what is immediately useful to the donor, as well as what will be useful to the library. He must also consider whether secondary or tertiary source materials are worth collecting if the library lacks basic records. Would they adequately support research? The attorney's case files and day books are vital; the writer's journals and drafts are more important to the researcher than the final version of a literary manuscript sent to the printer; the minister's sermon notes or manuscripts are useful if they are topical; the congressman's correspondence and subject files have much more significance than his patronage files or committee reports. Most emphasis should be placed on those original manuscript materials which reflect the individual and his creative or professional efforts. Did the creator keep journals or diaries? Did he retain the letters he received, as well as carbons of letters sent? Did he compile working notes or retain memoranda from each conference? Did he save minutes of meetings from civic or corporate boards? Did he make notes based on important telephone discussions?

MANUSCRIPTS

To the donor, a manuscript represents a neatly typed or handwritten document displayed under glass in a marble-walled museum, while to the librarian it has that broad definition which includes just about every type of handwritten or typed item, be it letter, diary, journal, map, draft, speech, article, note, or memorandum. The librarian must emphasize to the potential donor that his quest is broad and that the spontaneous, messy record is often more interesting than a final, polished document, perfect in every respect.

DIARIES AND JOURNALS

Perhaps most important to any library are good journals and diaries. A diary may record only weather, health, and food, but the librarian hopes it will contain personal detail and reflection. By its nature, a line-a-day diary becomes a record of the historically routine, uneventful aspects of an individual's life, and unfortunately, it has insufficient room to allow the writer to record his thoughts or to reflect upon them. The journal, on the other hand, is written at will, not holding the writer to a line-a-day or to a report on weather, ailments, and children. The journal is kept with much more detail, because its writer recognizes something special has occurred causing him to record or to reflect; the journal is a private record of emotions or events.

Both diary and journal represent to the donor the most sensitive, personal documents in his possession, and he may donate them only with some restrictions on use. A simple solution is for him to write a statement to be acknowledged by the library, indicating a specific period during which the records will be available to no one; of course, the shorter the period, the better. Ten, or a maximum of twenty, years should be adequate; or, should the donor's death occur before such a date, the material might then be released. The donor may place similar restrictions on an exchange of correspondence.

CORRESPONDENCE

Letters of all kinds kindle the enthusiasm of a librarian, whether they be personal, professional, business, or social. Best among them is often the long, continuous series in which the writer talks about himself or a special interest. These reflective letters can be written to a close relative, personal friend, or business associate. Surprisingly, the writer will often choose someone who is

not particularly close to serve as "father confessor." Our library has a series
written by the chief officer of a large Northwest lumber concern who
reported daily to the corporate board in Kansas City. His narrative letters
contain facts on production, sales, government controls, harvesting, cutting,
labor, administrative staff, market conditions, and so on. Another collection
contains an exchange of letters between Fred Glidden, a Western writer
better known by his pseudonym, Luke Short, and his literary agent, Marguerite
Harper, in New York City. Glidden talks of his creative successes and frustrations, while Miss Harper informs Glidden of the Western fiction market, sales,
trends, publishers, editors, and other agents. In both examples, the letters are
especially important, because the entire file exists, the letters cover a long
period of time, and they are written by experts within their field.

Professional correspondence, by its nature, discusses matters from an
educated, personal viewpoint, explaining the complexities and problems of
the profession, as well as exchanging gossip and fact about associates, present
trends, past history, and the future of the field. An exchange between
attorneys, ministers, writers, or architects shows each vocation in an in-depth
perspective. Letters to family, friends, old chums, or college classmates are
ignored by the donor, for he considers them to contain unimportant details
of personal life—child raising, marital problems, financial woes, family gossip.
In reality, these letters often contain personal assessment, commitment, or
comment concerning a special problem or project—the kind of frank statement
that would not appear in a more formal letter.

AUTOGRAPHS

Autograph letters are often over-rated, saved for the signature of the
writer but lacking in substantive content. In some cases, although the librarian
may not recognize the letter writer, he will realize that the donor prizes the
bland letter and its signature. The donor believes that the librarian and the
donor's heirs will battle over such precious documents; it is best, and most
tactful, to suggest that the letter remain with the family. On occasion, the
letter does have substance, and the librarian must make an individual decision.
He may suggest the donor retain the letter, while seeking permission to make
a copy for the donor's collection in the library. A purist claims that the original
letter ought to be given to the library and that the copy has diminished the
value of the letter itself, since its content is now public. Often the content of
the letter is such that the value is unaffected.

Other types of letters may have secondary importance to the library.
Fan letters to an actor, singer, writer, or artist often have little substantive
value. Pressure letters written by an organized group might well be considered

for possible sampling. Recent congressional files reflect the organized letter campaigns conducted by the anti-gun control lobby. The majority of letters were copied from one or more forms, or the form itself was sent to the politician. A sampling of such letters is usually sufficient. However, the spontaneous, intelligent, or enthusiastic letter recounting an individual's emotions or experience on the same subject should be retained. Fan letters, created as a public school project, reflect in their content the futility and disinterest in the project, and again may be sampled rather than retained as a unit.

In large political collections, as well as in other areas, the invitation, acknowledgment, and speaking date files may be heavily weeded. These letters rarely contain more than an appreciative sentence, as do appointments, confirmations, and transmittals. Such correspondence adds much bulk of questionable value to a large collection.

ADDRESS BOOKS

Address books, along with correspondence, become immediately useful to the librarian. Both contain information about other individuals of interest. The letters may introduce an excellent writer whose health has declined over the years; the address book may supply the names and addresses of his heirs. Letters are rarely written with an eye to the archivist, and thus last names and dates frequently are lacking. When assembling the collection, the dates may be transferred from the cancellation mark on the envelope, but without a return address or full signature, the letter should be set aside with the hope the final sort will provide the missing information. The address book may contain names of the subject, spouse, children, or other identification, which will help the librarian with the letter signed "Joe" or "Jo."

SPEECHES

Of lesser importance are written or recorded speeches, which reflect the public utterance and stance of the speaker but which may not indicate his personal opinion. Drafts of speeches or a series of speeches may indicate a change of thought or developing philosophy. The corporate manager, wavering politician, clergyman with doubts, or politically aspiring citizen may present a formal speech containing little that honestly reflects his personal thoughts. Tapes and videotapes present still another version of the speaker's public image.

PERSONAL FINANCES

Personal financial accounts are infrequently useful. A more consolidated form of financial accounting may have some value, but little emphasis need be placed on such records. The donor will usually worry about public access to his financial transactions, when, historically, the record is of little significance. The issue need not arise at all unless the librarian has a good reason to secure personal financial records.

PERSONAL MEMBERSHIP FILES

A civic-minded individual will retain minutes of meetings, speeches, and financial records from the various clubs and associations in which he participated. Such documents may be the only surviving records, especially when the secretarial position of the association rotated routinely. If the potential donor is a member of corporate boards, professional associations, or legislative or administrative bodies, minutes and similar records that he has retained should be assessed for possible value to the library.

SCRAPBOOKS

The creator may possess a series of scrapbooks: the first volume is carefully arranged with dates and all clippings mounted; the second volume contains unmounted, unrelated, undated clippings; the third has sheets ripped from the newspaper. As the subject became busier and engaged the spouse in more activities, the scrapbook project became less important. At best, scrapbooks contain stories about the positive contributions of the subject, for clippings detrimental to self-esteem are rarely retained. Thus, a series of scrapbooks may mean far more to the donor than to the library. It is better to refuse scrapbooks, suggesting their importance to the family and the researcher's genuine need to read all the newspapers of the period to catch the flavor of the time and those stories, which, in an absence from town, the clipper may have missed. Scrapbooks have a very short physical life, with poor glue, bad newsprint quality, and acid paperstock for the book itself. Occasionally, however, the scrapbook may contain some gems—a melange of clippings, letters, broadsides, and memorabilia.

BUSINESS AND CORPORATE RECORDS

What we have said about personal records is applicable to business or organization files. Key records include those which summarize activities, such as minute books, and those which narratively detail daily activities, such as outgoing correspondence arranged chronologically. Correspondence should be reviewed, because transmittals, references, invoices, and such can promptly be discarded. The business generally possesses a financial accounting system of daybooks, journals, or ledgers, which have special merit as a complete series, but, as a broken file, lack much value except as display samples.

SPECIALIZED RECORDS

Other materials may benefit a specialized collection. Artists, in addition to the desirable sketches, sketchbooks, and rough or finished art, maintain morgue files—subject picture files for research purposes. A librarian planning a picture file should consider the artist's morgue. The architect has his renderings, plans, correspondence, specifications, and drawings, as well as his reference library, professional journals, catalogs, construction photographs, site studies, and map files. The attorney may possess corporate records, minute books, and financial accounts of businesses unique to the region. In the Northwest, the local attorney's files may contain records of irrigation, livestock, ranching, mining, orchard, or lumber companies. His files, too, may include far better political or promotional materials than those of the politician or developer, for the advice for either campaign may stem from the attorney himself.

MANUFACTURERS' CATALOGS

A manufacturer's or dealer's catalog is a gem, but it is often ignored by both the donor and the librarian. Catalogs issued by jewelry, architectural, hardware, dental, medical, and industrial supply houses offer a record of the donor's era and work. They establish description, date, and price for many research projects. The promotional efforts of early catalogs and the current delight in nostalgia create a high interest today in such publications. If the business whose work is solicited issued its own catalogs, they represent an excellent record.

PHOTOGRAPHS

Most donors produce a formal, undated, studio portrait to be included with the collection for the benefit of the future user. The best photograph for a collection is an informal, well-identified, and dated one, which shows the subject engaged in his work or an avocation. Similarly, a series of photos of distant mountains or fields has much less use than a dated, identified picture of a local subject, building, farm, or familiar object. The old postal card photographer, who climbed the water tower to secure the community picture, performed a great historical service. His subject was clear and the card was well-identified as to place and date.

Construction photographs taken for an architect, contractor, or bank have far more interest and detail than the artistic angle shot of a local structure. The slide collection of a naturalist is welcome, but the occasional wildflower shot without location, date, and botanical name is as unimportant to the librarian as the poorly identified botanical specimen is to the botanist. To be of optimal use, photographs should be labeled with subject, place, and date. In emptying a photographic studio some years ago, we were plagued by kindly, elderly ladies from the community who wished to secure early photographs of themselves. As we delved deeper into the glass negatives, we discovered that the photographer had neither dated nor identified the subjects who posed for his nude studies. Occasionally, lack of identification is of definite advantage, at least to the subject of the study.

TRAVEL PHOTOGRAPHS, POSTCARDS, SLIDES

The traveler often collects everything readily available and takes photographs in the same inclusive manner, regardless of the subject. Photographs of distant places intrigue the donor, and he places considerable value on them; indeed, the librarian's time is often consumed while the donor tries to recollect the subject, time, and place of the photograph. Many photos and slides exist without identification, and, unless the donor has plenty of time and an excellent memory, ignore such unimportant records. The traveler with a good camera, an interest in keeping good records, and sufficient funds for good film and processing can supply the library with a splendid collection.

ORAL HISTORY

The donor is often prepared to relate his entire life history, and oral history is something to consider tentatively. Does the librarian have sufficient time and ability to conduct an interview, knwoledge to prepare the question to elicit information from the donor, staff to transcribe the tape and to retype the transcription after the donor has edited out what he feels inappropriate? What can the donor contribute to an oral history that is better than the contemporary written personal records placed in the library? Would a later informal interview conducted by the organizer of the gift be more appropriate for filling in the blank spots?

PRINTED MATERIALS

We have discussed types of manuscripts useful to a good collection, and most often the donor speaks first of this material. Meanwhile, the librarian with open eyes assesses, if possible, the book collection, which represents a more tangible asset to the donor. Although it is easier to consider only the immediate book needs of the library, with staff and shelf limitations a decided factor, the librarian must look to the future and select accordingly. The librarian has to have faith in his own judgment; he may believe that the library will collect the history of science, build its cookbook collection, begin an historical mystery section, or support new academic interest in the turn of the century popular American novel. Demand for such book collections develops within a college campus with little prior notice and with the expectation that the library will immediately provide cataloged books on the shelves without an increase in the book or processing budget.

PAMPHLETS

Pamphlets may be superb or hopeless, and it is only with experience that the librarian can begin to judge. A good subject collection is generally useful, if it is recent, or if it is so old that it is historical. Standard free items are sometimes unimportant, but the little newsprint pamphlet with limited distribution and an appeal to support or condemn an issue or individual may be exciting. Promotional, political, social, radical, conservative, and religious pamphlets ought to be examined carefully at the library, but not at the donor's home.

MAGAZINES

Of all published material, magazines and journals suffer most from time and exposure. They accumulate quickly and are usually poorly stored. In a moist basement or hot, dry attic, both paper and binding may deteriorate, and condition may be such that even a good run is of no consequence. Each librarian knows what his library needs, but he may also wish to suggest another library if he observes a good run of a duplicate title or one beyond the scope of his collection. If he knows the personnel of the suggested library, he might contact them himself, with the donor's permission. Much too often, periodicals are single issues, broken files, clipped, mutilated, and beyond any possible library value.

MISCELLANEOUS

Tucked on the donor's shelves may also be other library materials. Atlases and maps, whether current or old, automobile club, topographical, road and highway, engineering, aerial survey, or manuscript ought to be reviewed. Phonograph recordings may include old 78 rpms, as well as long-playing and tapes. What are the library's needs and will its collection take a new direction? Classical and popular sheet music seems to be a newly recognized collecting area in which lyricists, composers, graphic artists, and lithographers are now rediscovered.

Juvenilia can be interesting, especially if created by someone whose talents matured and whose adult creative work is a part of the library. Essays, poems, novels, and even a manuscript newspaper or cartoon series by the young, gifted individual will make good display material.

Whatever the material solicited, it should be authentic and complete. We recall one book collection of nineteenth century European history and, more vividly, the remarkable engravings on every wall of the home where the collection was stored. The owner of the library had removed the illustrated plates for use in his own home, for shows in public schools, for gifts to friends, and for sales to dealers. The value of the library was drastically diminished.

Chapter 4

SOURCES OF DONATIONS–LEADS

Perhaps the most zealously kept secret among librarians who seek manuscripts is the source of their donations, or "leads." Often the librarian feels that his leads are unique, his sources unknown and untried by others. And yet, each librarian has similar possibilities for access to leads and comparable means to secure sufficient information to ascertain current ownership of the potential gift. After all his efforts, he may find another librarian has already used the same processes to secure the desired material.

THE LIBRARY: A MAJOR SOURCE OF LEADS

The librarian has many assets in establishing the location of potential gifts. The library contains local, national, and international biographical dictionaries, professional directories, perhaps an index to the local or most important state-wide newspaper, and subject entries in the card catalog. The librarian can read journals and periodicals and use the proper indices to them. He can explore the library shelves or shelf list to identify the experts in given fields; he can observe the year of birth and sometimes the death date of the writer.

Users ask for addresses in order to write "fan" mail; the librarian needs to write fan letters, too, to those whose work he admires or whose work is important and whose materials would logically belong in the library. Are these potential donors of an age when they are ready to consider a donation or bequest, or should the library, in writing a younger person, suggest saving materials which will likely become important in the future? Is the creator of the collection deceased, and will the heirs reach a decision concerning the donation to the library?

APPLICATION TO TYPES OF LIBRARIES

The college librarian might well read about prospective donors in the alumni magazine; house organs and professional journals offer good subjects to the special librarian; the public librarian need only review announcements of local club meetings to consider possible organizations which span generations. A list of regional writers, musicians, or artists might appeal to the regional librarian. The architectural specialist might investigate the necrology in his professional journals, verify them against a biographical dictionary, and then act to make certain that files are saved rather than destroyed or dispersed. The academic librarian might explore a roster of fellows within a given discipline. Every library has its own interests, concerns, and attitudes toward specific fields of possible solicitation.

PROFESSIONAL LEADS

The librarian might consider what has happened to those sociologists, economists, or historians who were of national prominence but a few years ago. Are they still writing? Does a professional journal carry an obituary? Have they been dropped from a professional biographical dictionary or *Who's Who in America*, and if so, when did they last appear? Does *Who Was Who in America* or *The New York Times Obituary Index* contain an entry? If a subject was associated with an institution with a strong research library, his papers are probably already there; if not, a suggestion about preservation of the writer's library, manuscripts, working files, correspondence, and diaries is in order, after verifying the biographical information in several sources.

To secure enough information for a letter, the librarian might use many sources available in the library, ranging from *Biography Index* and *The National Cyclopedia of American Biography* to a local telephone book or an old city directory. Reference acumen is important. Once sufficient biographical material is available, a valid address for the subject or his heirs is the next step.

TELEPHONE DIRECTORIES

The telephone directory collection is vital, and an index to all cities for which the library has books is important. Too often a town or city is buried within a volume listed under the name of a neighboring town, district, or county unfamiliar to the librarian. Equally important, the librarian ought to employ an atlas to see if the subject's heirs have possibly moved to a nearby town, listed in a different telephone book.

CITY DIRECTORIES

While finding the donor may require a simple check in the telephone directory, location of an older collection or its owner may take much effort. An extremely useful tool is a series of city directories to verify the name of the subject, spouse's first name, vocation, and street address. All these bits of information are important, each in its own manner. By employing the reverse section of the city directory, arranged by streets, the librarian finds who lives in the old home now. Do any of the names suggest that the home is still owned by the family? If the occupant is listed as a widow, is it possible by use of the first name to assume that the individual was married to the subject sought? Has the widow remarried?—a clue would be that the occupant has the same first name as that listed earlier. If these possibilities exist, then the entire file of directories can be used to see when name changes took place and whether the theory is in fact correct. If the new occupant seems to have no relationship to the person sought, the librarian can contact the occupant, stating his purpose and asking for information about the former occupant; it is even possible that the former occupant might have left material in the attic.

SAMPLE APPLICATION

Checking a recent city directory against an older volume may show long family ownership within an established neighborhood. Such a situation occurred in a Northwest city; we admired several homes very much for their old architecture and the apparent large attics. Using the directories, we traced several generations of families and realized the types of material likely to be stored in the family homes. We contacted the owners, found that our estimates were correct, and two major collections became a part of our library.

The city directories supply basic information, and a good reference collection or newspaper index will produce the proper means of entrée by furnishing additional information.

NEWSPAPER FILES AND INDICES

Old newspaper files, especially when indexed, provide feature stories, obituaries, profiles, and articles that suggest individuals, businesses, or materials of interest. The newspaper index is very useful for local history, and an index to the largest newspaper in the state is nearly as helpful. For regional history, indices to several papers provide more information than most other sources; on a national basis, few published indices exist. *The New York Times Index* is indispensable, and *The New York Times Obituary Index*, which brings into one volume citations to all its obituaries through 1968, is priceless. The older the lead and the newspaper, the more detective work is necessary to locate the proper person to contact. The good newspaper index, with emphasis on personal and business names, and an inclusive obituary section, is a splendid aid.

The current newspaper, as well as providing a source for research, provides information about retirements, promotions, mergers, and corporate or personal deaths. Watching for similar news in other local media, as well as in periodicals and journals within the library's collecting scope, keeps the librarian current with possible leads.

When seeking material based on recent newspaper stories, the librarian feels often like a geriatric specialist or an ambulance- or hearse-chaser. The largest gifts may come from those who reach a time of life when collecting or saving is no longer important; at this point, potential donors may wish to divest themselves of material, and the library's expression of interest is an answer to their immediate problems. The move from a long-established family home to a retirement complex or nursing home means much to a library; at this time, files, letters, diaries, manuscripts, and books are dumped into the trash or scattered among friends or left in the attic for the next occupant's disposition.

Similar events included in current reading of newspapers and journals alert the librarian to possible leads. Does a law suit, divorce, bankruptcy, or bequest bring to mind a possible gift? Is it time to inquire about the material? Does marriage change the status of ownership? Does the formerly bereaved widow wish to dispose of her first husband's files now that she has remarried?

In traumatic events, a family lacks direction. In the most frank autobiography of a bookman with which we are familiar, Charles Everitt says that heirs and family members are suspicious of the collector in times of tragedy.

The librarian, however, may well appear as an informed, knowledgeable friend of the family, if he is sincere in his desire to cooperate with them.

Disposition of manuscripts often faces a family upon the death of the individual in whom the librarian is interested. The office, attic, basement, file room, closet, study, or storage area contain unknown records, and, at this emotional time, the family may destroy them, assuming that they are unimportant or of a purely personal nature. While the librarian might prefer to approach the living, creative individual, leads often derive from deaths. The librarian does read obituaries, but with considerable caution. The obituary may be a eulogy, written to please family and friends and to give its subject an appropriate send-off in his final venture. Details of position, accomplishment, and abilities are frequently exaggerated. An obituary provides vital statistics and identifies family members, but it must be used thoughtfully.

MUG BOOKS

A "mug book" contains a version of the eulogy, but it is written while the subject is still alive. A self-supporting or vanity publication, the mug book is based on the inclusion of portraits and paid biographies. Most historians view the local or state mug book with considerable skepticism, but the librarian welcomes information concerning family background, heirs, and dates. Armed with this data, he can turn to the city directory or the telephone book to locate current heirs.

CLIPPING FILES

Many libraries maintain personal name indices to regional mug books. The same file may include historical or biographical clippings and citations to standard publications. The library may possess a similar file created from dust jackets and other sources with biographical information about authors. If the librarian collects literary manuscripts, he has a ready source of data, probably located close to the standard tools for literary biographies, *Contemporary Authors*, *Twentieth Century Authors*, and *American Authors and Books*. Many special libraries maintain similar biographical vertical files or indices in their particular subject matter.

THE LIBRARY'S OWN FILES

The library office contains a good source for future leads; correspondence with former donors ought to be reviewed very carefully for leads and tactical errors, too. An oversight by the library may have left the donor unhappy and still in possession of good materials. Many contacts ought to be revived, either with a direct inquiry about further donations or with a suggestion that advice and support would be welcomed. It may be embarrassing to return to a donor who once offered a collection now in a much desired field; the librarian ought to swallow his pride and ask. If a former donor no longer makes gifts, the librarian should learn the reasons from the donor or library associates. The librarian may discover that a former donor has died but that the library has neglected to ask his family for the remainder of his work or the last portion of a gift begun years ago.

We emphasize the unhappy former donor; as a new staff member or one in a new position, the librarian can manifest a fresh interest in the donor's concerns and complaints, once the librarian makes certain the library has not discarded the earlier donation or donations. Complaints about handling of gifts are often valid in libraries where gift acquisition has not been assigned to a specific staff member. Perhaps the librarian can rectify the wrong, please the donor, and elicit further gifts or information about other collections.

MANUSCRIPT COLLECTIONS

Manuscript collections secured as gifts provide a wide variety of leads. By reading the correspondence files, the librarian discovers book collectors, offspring with family papers, associates whose letters rival in quality those within the collection, libraries seeking disposition of collections, incisive discussions concerning disputes or personalities. In each case, with knowledge secured from the original gift, the librarian seeks out supporting gifts, or gifts that may surpass the collection in hand. He notes those people with ability to write well, with special talent for serious criticism or analysis, with sound knowledge of their specialty, or with privileged information.

ASSOCIATES AND FRIENDS

The librarian has within his grasp the silent manuscript and printed sources as leads to potential donations. He also has the opportunity to apply similar techniques of detection when he works among people and associations—library staff, associates, clubs, neighbors, friends, and relatives. In addition to leads, these individuals may have special ties with the prospect or have some personal knowledge which would help with the negotiations. Did they attend college with the spouse, establish friendship through children, encounter the tyrant with whom no one gets along? Forearmed with bits of personal information, the librarian may phrase a more suitable letter or find the initial visit far easier.

An acquaintance of the prospective donor, or a business or professional associate, can often help with the donor, family, heirs, or friends. It is better to be direct with this agent, to indicate why the library seeks the individual or his family. Occasionally, a good soul will protect the subject from such inquiry, believing that the librarian represents a collection agency or sales promotion concern. "Considering the source" is important in talking with friends; some advice is far less objective and accurate than what is already at hand in the library.

The ability to recognize useful help comes from carefully evaluating suggestions. Too many "helpful" people refer the librarian to other "friendly" people, people who never saved, have little interest, lack specific knowledge, are unwilling to share information, and cost the librarian considerable time. Evaluation of suggestions, of those who make them, and of their understanding of the library's program is critical, if one is not to lose days and weeks in social calls.

Over the years, we have found one consistently poor source for leads, names, heirs, and addresses. He is the "colorful character." The character seldom corresponded, and his legendary knowledge seems constructed in the newspaper office on slack days. His home was often a rooming house, his income non-existent, and he left little graphic record. The colorful character spent his lifetime weaving stories without foundation or documentation.

DONORS

Interested donors often become the library's best representatives, watching for materials, speaking on the library's behalf, and informing the librarian of suggested action. One banker urged his professional associates and most distinguished friends to place their working files and books in our library. Another banker, a trust officer, made certain that the library's interests were considered when any estate held unassigned books or manuscripts. An economics professor, whose wife did not want books to clutter her home, systematically gathered books as his hobby to strengthen our library. A retired alumnus regularly purchased late nineteenth century fiction, which he mailed to the library. Students who noted the weakness of special areas have bought appropriate materials. The attorney who faces an estate with problems of storage, disposition, and taxes may seek the librarian, if previous negotiations have been agreeable. The retirement home, the apartment hotel, the local mover all provide sources for leads. In each situation, an interested library friend can inform the librarian of a projected move, a new event which may call for a change in lifestyle. The librarian's friends, representatives, or spies located in strategic spots are important for new leads.

One of our finest book gifts came from a large apartment complex, from which all traces of our lead had disappeared. We spoke with the manager, who introduced us to the senior resident. We explained our purpose in seeking the former resident and were told how the collection had been dispersed. However, with a glass of sherry in hand, our new potential donor told us we were welcome to select whatever we wished from her four-thousand-volume library. Not only did the new donor answer our question and make a substantial donation to the library, but she became a source of neighborhood information, providing support in winning hard-to-secure collections.

BOOK DEALERS

The knowledgeable used book or antiquarian dealer's assistance and leads can be very useful, if the library cooperates fairly with the bookseller. Will he disclose leads with which he has not been successful? He may have been offered a collection for appraisal; its owner may find the figure too low, wish to keep the collection intact, or desire tax benefit rather than sale. The dealer sometimes lacks sufficient information to locate an heir, whom the library resources locate quickly. Will the bookman refer to the library a collection that is in an area of its interests but not within his own specialties? Using political and physical resources of the library and his access to community friends, can the librarian verify the bookman's rumor of a vast collection and solicit the material or inform the dealer? A clear understanding of how the librarian plans to use the dealer's leads is important to a good working relationship.

Librarians often consider that the second-hand bookman lacks the librarian's professional expertise, but the dealer does make his living from the buying and selling of materials. The librarian ought to consider his book friend a true associate and refer appropriate book problems to the dealer. He does not recommend a seller with an impossible collection of "dogs" (books of no value to anyone), since each negotiation takes the dealer's time, and and the dealer's regard for the librarian who recommends worthless collections diminishes. If he directs a collection to the dealer, the librarian informs the dealer of the reasons for the referral. Too many librarians have poor relationships with dealers, because it has been easier to send poor material to a dealer than to refuse it for the library. A successful bookman does not survive by selling junk, nor does the librarian merit the dealer's respect when the librarian has given the prospective seller a casual or exaggerated financial estimate of value.

COLLECTORS

In his library and the bookshop, the librarian may learn of collectors. Manuscript or book collectors are the librarian's ultimate pleasure. Each has given to his one specialty all those things which the librarian cannot afford to give: commitment, time, funds, expertise, patience, and drive. Each knows far more about his subject than the librarian does, or will, and the librarian ought to have the interest and patience to learn. The collector knows his field—the best writers, scarcest books, best second-hand dealers, recognized publishers, local specialists, and key bibliographies.

The expert may have an unbridled passion for his specialty. Thus, he can become a burden to the library, as can any donor. Upon presentation of the gift, he may come to see what the library is doing, who is using the gift, how the gift is housed, and whether the gift is supported with current purchases, adequate staff, and appropriate maintenance. From the library's point of view, the best collector or donor, in general, is the one whose interest has turned toward another field, or who moves to a retirement home where space prohibits further collecting.

BLANKET SOLICITATION

Many libraries pursue a field intensively, employing various professional directories. Such leads are considered "blind" leads, for, indeed, the librarian lacks knowledge of the potential donors, except the biographical material before him. A careful record of such blanket mailings, names, and locations is essential, for otherwise one potential donor may receive three letters, his name having appeared in three vocational directories. The forms may be identical, or, if he appears in a professional directory, a regional who's who, and in *Who's Who in America*, the content of the letter may be slanted in different directions. A poorly conducted blanket form letter campaign, without careful consideration of the leads and careful maintenance of lead files, is an embarrassment to the library. On the other hand, a thorough examination of a new biographical directory, compared with an older volume, shows those subjects who are no longer active or who are deceased; such subjects often are potential leads to the imaginative librarian.

Collections useful to the library exist in both obvious and unexpected places. The librarian who gives consideration to these suggestions and then examines his own library's needs and resources ought to see where he might solicit donations for his library, provided others have not trod in the same vineyard.

Chapter 5

CORRESPONDENCE

The most important part of a manuscript solicitation program is the librarian's relationship with the donor, established by letters and visits. The initial letter identifies the library and introduces the librarian as its personal representative, interested in the potential donor's specialty. A poorly phrased letter, with incorrect grammar, current jargon, or library-oriented terminology, may offend the donor. The letter is written to a specialist, an educated person, who may well be advanced in years and who is always deserving of respect. The letter should not be created in a burst of enthusiasm and admiration, but it should contain a well-considered suggestion, based on specific reasons for seeking the gift and on knowledge of the potential donor.

THE FIRST LETTER

The initial letter explains something about the institution, its special collections, the purposes for which it has gathered and maintained collections, and the reasons for writing the letter. A sincere letter is more effective than a form with one or two blanks to personalize the content. A letter created on a machine, such as the flexiwriter or Mag Card I, reflects the impersonality of the machine and a collecting program similar to direct mail advertising, with the recipient's name included at several points in the letter. Contemporary advertising techniques are all too familiar, and a genuine letter from an intelligent librarian is a welcome change.

The first letter should display an interest in the potential donor and ask for a response. The letter does not push, shove, or coerce. The recipient learns of the institutional program or what the library is doing; he reads of the library's present and long-range plans to implement the program; he discovers the reasons for the importance of the project; and lastly, he realizes what he may contribute in the way of materials. As one donor wrote, "Your letter is the only one I have received which makes sense." Too many libraries contact a prospective donor with an all-inclusive, unimaginative form letter, or a poorly planned and ill-constructed plea for tokens or souvenirs. Should a library ask for the writer's book, or should it consider, too, his library, his working files, his correspondence, and the entire body of creative effort assembled by the writer? The answer depends upon the library and its collecting purposes.

The letter needs to be written to the donor, not to a wide spectrum of potential donors. It should mention specifically the creative person's work, his association with others whose manuscripts the library has, his contributions to specific groups or organizations, his publications, and similar personal detail. The catch-all letter is simply that—it appeals to everyone to donate anything and everything. Its scope is so broad that it sounds like an appeal for a trash cleanup.

Some libraries use assorted letterheads to catch the eye of the donor and to create the impression that the institution collects only in a specific field. Without a good control file, which lists all donors and potential donors, the recipient is likely to possess two or three forms with different letterheads, appealing to the creative person for his Western ranching records, his library of Americana, and his contemporary political files. Sincerity is a far better approach, for the donor has friends with similar interests, and from them he learns of the receipt of identical letters with identical letterheads. The program becomes either an amusement among those solicited or a serious concern centered on possibly dubious motivation of the library. Such letter writing, generally produced by a machine typewriter, casts a very fine net to include all possible fish—large and small, good and not so good. The results of such a catch may cause more problems than benefits: did the librarian seek a local newspaper poet, a regional poet whose two slim volumes were self-published, or only poets of national stature?

The initial or subsequent letter explains the strengths of the library, its resources—newspapers, journals, books, and manuscripts within the special field and period of the donor. Reference should be made to the present and future users of the material and to possible means of sharing the information with users elsewhere through cooperative manuscript publications, such as the *National Union Catalog of Manuscript Collections*. The letter should introduce the manuscripts curator and stress how well the collections are organized, housed, and used, with specific information.

An enthusiastic or emotional appeal, written with a burst of energy and spirit, usually fails in its effort. That letter often pleads for any scrap of paper, which is what is elicited from the donor—scraps of paper, something to satisfy the request. The emotional appeal to support a library struck by flood, fire, or other disaster, provokes the same type of gift—anything. Those shelves are bare and the donor wants to provide whatever is at hand—good, bad, and terrible. The need to sort and discard a large portion of materials thus secured requires a major expenditure of time and staff.

A poorly structured initial appeal can ramble, repeating minor points; it may never reach the direct request for material. The recipient wonders why the letter was written and whether its writer is an individual capable of managing a special collection. Repetition and rephrasing of facts already stated merely waste the reader's time. The initial appeal, the librarian should remember, is to an intelligent person.

The letter should not overwhelm the donor with a verbal barrage of facts; details appear in later letters, when the librarian responds to the donor's questions. Mention of associates whose files already exist in the library and inclusion of a good inventory to serve as an example provide effective information to the donor, pointing out that here are other collections related to his, well-organized and available for use. Several examples of initial letters appear in the Appendices 5-1, 5-2, and 5-3.

We receive responses to more than half our first letters, the result probably due to the quality and tone of the letters. We have been surprised by letters of similar intent sent by other libraries, letters which presuppose that the donor should be flattered by the institution's interest and honored to be preserved in its great archives.

An immediate response to the first letter may not be forthcoming. Some of our letters, written as far back as 1959, still elicit an initial response, often from an heir who finds our letter in a safety deposit box or among personal instructions or even in a pile of unanswered letters. It is hardly possible to keep a file active for fifteen or more years without some response, but it is important to keep a record that the library has made inquiry.

THE FOLLOW-UP LETTER

While we receive considerable response to our initial letters, we realize that many people do not write letters without effort. If no reply is received, we send a second letter six weeks or two months later, in order to elicit a response. The return from the second letters is again almost half, although included in this count are letters with improper addresses. The second letter is written with no knowledge of the potential donor's reaction to the library's initial suggestion; response to the second letter usually indicates that the recipient has not received the first letter, has misplaced it, or simply has not taken time to respond. The second letter contains a gentle reminder that the library is interested in the collection and would welcome word from the recipient. An example of the letter appears as Appendix 5-4.

Many libraries write but one letter to a prospective donor. Apparently the recipient must respond immediately or he is no longer of interest. Perhaps the letter is written with an enthusiasm that later flags, and the collection becomes unimportant to the library. Because we write a second, reminder letter, our library has secured many collections that had previously been solicited by other institutions.

POSITIVE AND NEGATIVE DONOR RESPONSE

Initiation of correspondence is designed to provoke a response leading to a donation. However, other replies are very useful, from an expression of possible interest to knowledge of disposition of the material. Was the collection lost by fire or flood, distributed among relatives, or given in its entirety to another institution? As time passes, the need to keep a record of such disposition becomes more and more evident; the librarian and researcher both need to know whether a collection ever existed and whether there is still access to it within a family or institution. As the librarian works to build a subject specialty, does he notice a pattern? Was the gift solicited by another library already interested in the same materials? Was it given locally and really thrust upon a none-too-willing recipient? Was it given to the subject's alma mater? What does the librarian know of that institution's collection? Would the gift be a burden to that institution? If so, would the recipient be willing to pass it along to the collecting library? Too often, the librarian learns that the individual never saved his working files, or that they remained at the office, or that they were given to a junior member of the firm, who later destroyed them as ancient history.

THE CORRESPONDENCE FILE:
AN HISTORICAL RECORD OF THE GIFT

It is useful to have a written record of all negotiations with the donor. The personal visit, which may result from the correspondence, becomes an opportunity for the librarian to assess the collection and its donor, and for the donor in turn to assess the library and its representative. With the library's purpose, philosophy, policies, and interest already expressed by letter, the potential donor does not have misconceptions about the donation and the visit may well conclude the negotiations for the gift.

Subsequent letters, which confirm and reaffirm those statements made during meetings, need to possess the same sincerity apparent in the first letter. It is better to have everything in writing than to have oral agreements with which the librarian's successor and/or the donor's heirs are unfamiliar.

The correspondence files become key records for gifts solicited as well as for gifts received. All the negotiations, formal and informal, are summarized in the correspondence, from the initial contact to confirmation of what occurred during the visits. The initial letter that provokes a positive response almost always leads to the librarian's direct visit to the home or office of the potential donor.

Chapter 6

VISITING THE DONOR

With the potential contributor's interest aroused and a possible gift in the offing, the librarian is anxious to see the material and to talk with the donor. It is time to arrange a meeting to assess both the material and its owner.

PHYSICAL PRESENCE

The initial meeting is better arranged by letter than by telephone. The prospective donor can too easily refuse or postpone a meeting during a telephone conversation. The call does not provide him sufficient time to reflect on whether he is ready for a personal meeting, unless he has suggested that the librarian should arrange a date. A letter from the librarian, which sets a specific appointment, allows the donor ample opportunity to decide whether he wishes the meeting.

The librarian's visit indicates a personal and institutional interest, not just someone at the distant end of a letter. Our library has received many collections because we sent a representative; other libraries had written inquiries but had made no personal contact. A conservatively dressed librarian with good presence is reassuring; the apparent implication is that the institution and its representative will treat the donation with respect. We have encountered many situations where the gift was promised by mail, the material was already packed for shipment, and yet the owner had to reassure himself of the sincerity of the request. The visit took several minutes of conversation, and the gift was consummated. The difference between the visit and letter at that point is one of securing the donation; few libraries attempt to meet the potential donor. This is especially true among academic institutions.

The visit allows each individual to take his measure of the other. The donor may ask questions about the library, its program, and the reasons for seeking his materials. The librarian can make a personal evaluation of the donation being offered and of the contributor.

ASSESSING THE DONOR

Librarian and donor are equally nervous about the meeting, and the concerned librarian ought to allow the donor to talk. Most often the donor initiates the conversation, and much can be learned by listening rather than repeating orally what the librarian has already clearly stated by letter. A good listener discovers what items have been scattered, sold, or destroyed; what restrictions the potential benefactor may wish to place on the contribution; what institution has been offered the gift after being informed of the impending visit (very often the donor will contact his local library, either to ask if it wishes his material, or as a gesture of derision; if the library is caught unawares, it often pleads that it has been expecting the gift and is ready to receive it); which family members now want to divide the materials among them, so that each may have a remembrance. The librarian listens, too, to make certain the contributor has a good conception of the library's interests, to learn whether the gift's importance is only in the donor's eyes, and to prepare himself for later discussion.

The donor educates the librarian about the specialty—major books, recent trends, and new or historical leaders. The librarian, as an attentive listener, is engaged in a tutorial session, not a sales meeting. His host may ignore matters of concern to the library or may mention friends with similar collections. The librarian stays alert, though the monologue rambles, digresses, and never returns to the original point. It is better to be attentive first, and then lead the speaker or draw him out with good questions.

Frequently, the librarian has just stepped over the threshold when the monologue begins and the solicitor accepts the handiest chair. If possible, it is helpful to isolate an interest shared by the donor. Does he have antiques, a Siamese cat, an unusual piece of furniture, or an evident hobby? By establishing a personal rapport, the librarian may receive a tour of the home or office, which provides a chance to see the material under discussion, as well as items which may never have entered the donor's mind as something of use to the library. The tour may include the attic, basement, closets, and the study—possible locations of books or files about which the alert librarian will ask, if they do not appear to be part of the gift.

THE LIBRARIAN'S ROLE

Just as he has carefully phrased his letters, the librarian considers his response to the donor's questions and underlying thoughts. While listening, he has selected those points to which to respond directly; he provides an answer to each but does not belabor these responses. An attempt to provide the same answer in three different ways is unwarranted. However, he informs the donor of his intention to confirm the discussion in his next letter.

The librarian should try to avoid more than the social cup of tea or coffee while conducting the negotiations, since luncheon, special guests, and social amenities detract from the matter at hand. It is helpful if the librarian is not confined to the listener's chair for the course of a meal or because others are anxious to meet this interesting librarian. The librarian wants as little socializing as possible on this first visit, so that he may see and assess the potential gift.

As the representative of the library, the librarian's manner, diplomacy, and social conversation are important. His willingness to assist in moving cartons, to accept household dust, to pack a carton or two for the donor's use, to straighten the shelves he empties, to crawl into the dark attic to move the books, and to express interest in the owner's children or pets again demonstrates the librarian's concern for the donor and his material. Also, by helping, the librarian has a chance to watch for cartons or files that have escaped the donor's notice. The contributor is intent upon what he feels is important to the institution. The librarian's watchful concern may lead to associated material to enrich the gift.

Meetings provide a variety of experiences, some pathetic, many enjoyable, and a few thoroughly humorous. The creative person, the creator of those files sought by the library, is generally an enjoyable, informed individual who has agreed to share with others the problems and successes he has encountered in his field. The widower or widow, on the other hand, may have little knowledge of the spouse's work, and the emotional strain of the meeting is evident. Such persons are anxious either to dispose of everything quickly or to retain it forever. In the latter case, the librarian tries to secure permission to view the precious remains, for often that reverence later gives way without warning to wholesale housecleaning.

The survivor is often concerned about some indiscretion, financial problem, or family matter; he believes the files are "too personal" to place in a public institution. Will the removal of the personal files lead to a completely dehumanized collection, bowdlerized beyond hope? The librarian might accept that personal section under seal for a period of years; he could stress the research value of having all the files, not just those which show the individual in a positive light; or, in other situations, he may decide that the segment or the entire collection is not worth preservation.

Offspring of the creative person occasionally seem unaware of the reasons for outside interest; the deceased was viewed only in a parental or avuncular relationship, with little understanding of his contributions to society at large. Such offspring may retain everything, perhaps the result of having shown no appreciation for the parent while he was alive, or in the expectation that the material will sell at a remarkable price, or more rarely, from a genuine interest. If materials have survived for several generations, the heirs usually have a broader view of the research value and may be willing to share their records by placing them in the library. One lament heard from succeeding generations is that the grandfather never appears in history books; the reason may be simply that the family papers were dispersed or destroyed, or that they remained in private ownership.

Fortunately, it is only infrequently that the librarian encounters a bore or boor with little to donate and hours arranged to entertain and show off his visitor. On the other hand, at the end of a long day the librarian may meet a tearful widow, a distressed daughter, an angry businessman, a senile gentleman, or a donor turned salesman. A car provides the easiest physical escape, or an invented appointment elsewhere may furnish an excuse for rapid departure. He should not, however, indicate at the outset of the meeting the existence of further dates; some latitude in the schedule should be allowed. If he feels hurried, the donor either rushes to tell the librarian everything and forgets the most important thing (to permit the librarian to examine the possible donation) or he so belittles his material that the librarian does not see it. It is difficult to estimate the length of an initial visit, but we generally expect to spend about an hour—the first half hour listening with a hope that the collection may be of interest, the second half hour looking at the material and evaluating the donor, the gift, and its availability.

The librarian may feel pressed to take an unwanted collection because the donor is about to burst into anger or tears. If so, the librarian can accept the collection tentatively, suggesting that he wishes to review it in detail (while knowing full well that he will return it). Accepting a certain amount of unwanted material is part of the collecting process, but having the option of return understood provides the library with an easy solution. By laying groundwork, too, the librarian ought to build his conversation in order to refuse an inappropriate gift, perhaps with a suggestion of a more suitable location for the material.

A second library worker is always helpful during initial meetings and later in packing sessions. The staff member assists with conversation, acts as observer (what did the donor really say or mean), and takes notes. When it is time to pack and haul, one worker may well engage the donor in conversation in order to free his associate. The associate packs, undisturbed by the donor's questions, comments, or need to review each piece of paper. Again, two library representatives are better equipped to assume the burden of conversation in cases of emotional stress. The donor may witness the examination or packing of the deceased partner's files, a situation quite similar to removal of a casket, and an immediate diversion from an emotional situation is important; discussion of the objects noted on the house tour, that common bond shared with the donor, or the librarian's special interest in the gift itself may provide the relief needed.

If the initial meeting takes place without preceding correspondence, the librarian identifies the institution for which he is soliciting, the reasons for collecting, and his interest in talking with the potential donor. He provides the donor with his full name, address, and telephone number (perhaps a calling card). He confirms the meeting with a letter which relates all the points discussed. Such a situation occurs when a satisfied donor introduces the librarian to a friend or friends, perhaps in an apartment house or retirement home. The friend has only heard of the donor's satisfaction and has gleaned some impression of the library, program, and librarian. The new prospective donor deserves a letter of clarification.

SORTING AND PACKING

The librarian brings to the donor's home flat, folded cartons, shipping labels, and staples. A staple gun transforms the flat cartons into shipping boxes, and filament tape seals them. A good marking pen identifies the contents to help when the shipment arrives at the library. With these materials, the librarian does not waste time searching for supplies, and packing becomes a routine operation.

By doing his own sorting and packing, the librarian shows the donor the interest and care which the manuscripts will receive in the library. The same process allows the librarian to consider the materials against the needs of the entire library. What does the library really need; which things might it possibly use; and how much is totally inappropriate?

In addition to the library's needs, the librarian considers condition—dry rot, mildew, silverfish, mice litter, or water damage. Have the ravages of time destroyed the material? He watches for obvious gaps in the gift and calls them to the donor's attention: where are the missing records? It is far better to pack all the material than to learn later what was missed through oversight.

He watches, too, for associated materials, such as bookkeeping textbooks to explain the firm's antique accounting system, shorthand books to decipher the secretary's notebooks, the file clerk's manual or key to the filing system, or the professional journal in which the subject's early articles appear. The importance of the donor's library is obvious, but his special tools are often neglected. Does the donor have an old-fashioned recording or tape machine which will be needed in order to play those discs?

If apparent order exists in the files, the librarian packs in sequential order, noting the alphabetical breaks on both the inside and exterior of the carton. The files can then be reconstructed easily in the library. If there is only a broad subject order, based on a shelf or two of files that have some similarity, a note to that effect is helpful.

While it may seem superficially reasonable to sort at the donor's home or office in order to return to the library with an organized collection, there are several excellent arguments against such a plan. The librarian would need an appropriate place to work and perhaps some reference tools; the donor would distract and delay his work by offering social amenities and the usual questions or conversation; per diem expenses would become a necessity; and, in the case of unorganized, associated materials, it would be very difficult to pick and choose among them without having made a thorough organization of the basic gift. Only with space, time, and staff does the arrangement become apparent, and, at that point, the material falls into order or into the discard pile.

Freight or postal costs are minor when compared to the time necessary for a careful sort at the donor's home. It may well be easier to take everything offered, with the understanding that the library will make appropriate disposition of unwanted materials. Such disposition, the librarian suggests, includes adding the material to other sections of the library, offering it to other libraries, sending it to libraries abroad, exchanging it for credit with dealers, or destroying it. Only occasionally does the donor wish to have the library return whatever it does not retain.

A tactful way of leaving or refusing unwanted materials is helpful when there are large segments of obviously impossible materials. They may be of special value to the donor or his family, the librarian can suggest, or, if he does see potential use by another library, he will mention that library, and later make contact with it himself.

It is advantageous for the librarian to sort and pack. The professional mover or packer often disregards existing file order, filling the empty spaces in each carton with no thought to the later problems of organization. The donor might be shocked by the mover's disrespect of the materials and therefore plan no further gifts, and the librarian who receives a shipment packed by movers might be overwhelmed by the chaos.

SHIPMENT OR PHYSICAL TRANSFER TO THE LIBRARY

While packing and sorting may seem like menial jobs, even more so is hauling material to the car or wagon in which the librarian has arrived. The donor will rarely move the carton from his home to the library or a shipping point, and the librarian must plan the transfer himself. Carrying cartons and labels and then packing the gift expedites the shipment. If the shipment is ready to be picked up by a freight company but remains a few days at the donor's, the donor may have second thoughts about the gift. His children, associates, and friends all have better suggestions, he discovers, than the librarian who packed the material. Why not send it to the local library, present it to the donor's old college, lend it to a relative who plans to write the donor's biography, or sell it to the local second-hand furniture and bookstore? The librarian shudders at those suggestions, but we have lost an occasional gift because we were unable to move the shipment immediately upon packing it. If at all possible, the cartons should be removed from the donor's home or office.

Financially, it costs less for the librarian to do his own packing than to have a mover do the job, and, in addition, the gift is secured, not simply awaiting a mutually convenient time when the donor and shipper can meet. The librarian should arrive at the donor's with several possibilities for shipment in mind: will the librarian take the boxes to a nearby post office spotted en route, or to the shipper whose address he obtained from his local freight company, or to the library itself, if it is not too distant? Using the postal service library rate is by far cheapest, but truck or freight companies are reasonable and often provide prompter service. The professional mover is a last resort; his service is expensive and, for a distant shipment, the elapsed shipping time is longer than mail or motor freight.

BOOK COLLECTIONS

While this text deals with manuscript solicitation, the good book collection is often a concurrent gift, available for the asking. As the librarian examines the manuscripts, he observes the books, especially if they are of interest to the library. Frequently, the donor's intent becomes apparent as the librarian listens: the donor may wish the librarian to take all, to select specific volumes, or to admire the collector's pride and joy. The librarian's personal delight, amazement, or enthusiasm may leave him speechless, which is advisable as the donor talks of his plans for the books. The librarian should avoid giving voice to his enthusiasm in terms of a financial value based on an immediate impression.

The book collection may be beneath library calibre, and in this case it is difficult to believe that those books have supported the donor's work. The librarian remains silent while charting a course to avoid having to take the books. Does the donor have some pet school which might use the books? Are his children pursuing his field of interest? Should the books be retained within the family as antiques? The librarian listens with the hope the donor himself will supply the solution.

The good personal library may still be of use to the donor. The librarian may suggest specific items for immediate library needs, or select a few lesser items to serve as a down payment against a future major gift, thereby establishing the library's interest and the donor's intent. When selection from a good personal collection becomes a matter of book-by-book discussion, it is better for the librarian to withdraw; he is wasting his time and the donor's.

However, if the donor is cordial and in a giving mood, consider the interests of the entire library. Does the library need to replace a well-worn classic, secure a second copy of a heavily used reference tool, include another copy of a best-seller on the new book shelves, complete a broken file of a periodical, anticipate the demand for a local historical pamphlet, or store a copy of the item so often stolen from the shelf? The librarian does not deliberate when the donor is in a giving frame of mind; the librarian acts.

COMMITMENTS

In accepting a gift of books or manuscripts, the library has committed itself to the donor as well as to the gift. The manuscript collection is received for the life of the institution unless the terms of the gift are spelled out otherwise. The commitment, too, includes arrangement according to library or archival practice and proper protection and use within intellectual confines agreeable to the library and donor. Librarians who profess in this era of freedom of access that the donor has no further influence or control over his donation are literally correct, but, in reality, the misuse of a collection easily becomes front-page newspaper copy and ruins the chance for receipt of further gifts.

Commitments radiate in many directions. Will the donor haunt the library, supervise the collection, and take staff time? By accepting the gift, has the library subscribed to the donor's political, religious, or philosophical beliefs? Has the library deprived the donor of an immediate cash sale, which, in his tenuous financial situation, looks advantageous? Is the donor motivated by tax purposes, seeking an exorbitant appraisal? If the gift is to a college library, does the donor seek an honorary degree or readmission of his delinquent offspring? Does the donor wish an office in the library, a memorial room, an assistant, a formal position, an instant biography, or a printed catalog? These questions may arise in the librarian's mind on rare occasions, but he should be prepared to face them when he evaluates the donor and the potential gift.

DIARY AND FIELD NOTES

After every visit, whether it be the first or a return visit, the librarian must take time to make notes about the meeting. What did the gift include, and how was it organized? What was lacking, and why was it withheld? Did the donor mention other collections? Did he speak of friends in possession of his work? Should the librarian return? What family members should become a part of the social exchange between the librarian and donor in the future? What has the library to offer the donor which would please him? The next letter or a future visit will be much easier with notes from the previous meeting. In a day when six or eight meetings take place, the librarian's diary helps him to recall the prospective donors and their possible gifts.

A collection may be scattered by and among two or three succeeding generations. Listening to the donor and taking notes provide clues as to who now possesses what; notes kept on the spot place the several generations of heirs in perspective. The librarian will pursue the leads, but the donor will find other things to do and may lack the cordial family relationship to reach all branches. Field notes are precious and should be copious. Another suggested record of the initial meeting appears as Appendix 6.

MISTAKES

As the librarian learns to meet donors, he makes mistakes. He accepts too much or takes too little; he is overwhelmed by family relationships; he allows too much time for a hopeless donor or too little for a promising potential donor. In nervousness, he may repeat all those facts emphasized in his letter, or he may enjoy the sound of his voice as he reiterates those statements which he had composed in the library. He may need the reassurance of a briefcase, full of photographs of his library and its collections, with accompanying testimonial letters from satisfied donors. The hard sell is not necessary and resembles the salesman's emphatic pitch for the purchase of a cemetary lot. Indeed, it is the individual's work, not the individual, that will be preserved in the library.

With experience, the librarian learns, in those first visits, to let the donor talk rather than to repeat the statements already made in a letter. The donor has been waiting for the librarian, waiting to tell him about his career and the materials he has gathered. The librarian presents a new audience for those stories which are too familiar to family and friends. The donor needs to talk. If the librarian talks and talks, he loses the potential donor and the collection.

RULES OF THUMB

We have met nearly ten thousand potential donors over twenty years and have developed several theories. The smaller the individual's accomplishments, the more unwilling he is to share them with others. The harder the librarian works to see or secure a collection, the less significant it will be and the less likely the library is to receive it. Small attorneys in whose control a client's papers are placed create every possible reason to retain them; successful attorneys seize upon the library as an excellent, legitimate repository. The potential donor who immediately refers the librarian to others with better collections rarely has a collection himself; that donor's suggestions are poor and are offered simply to fend off the librarian. The old local sage has little except pithy sayings and a remarkable reputation; he lacks substantive records.

Chapter 7

RECEIPT, SORTING, ORGANIZATION, DESCRIPTION, AND FINANCIAL APPRAISAL

With a gift in hand, or, more specifically, in the rear of the station wagon or the back of a truck, the librarian's obligations begin seriously. The excitement of the chase is over, but a new intellectual process commences. What does the librarian have? How will he assemble it to make it available to present and future scholars? How will he store it? What did the donor withhold because he had not yet reviewed it, had loaned it to a friend, found it too sensitive, or planned to use it to his own purpose? Will the gift be arranged immediately or in a year or two, due to lack of space or staff or because other collections will be processed ahead of it? What notes will be necessary now to expedite the arrangement later?

RECEIPT OF GIFT FORM

Presenting the donor an official receipt at the time the gift is made reassures him that it is now formal library property. The receipt includes a general description of the material (i.e., twelve cartons of correspondence, memoranda, books, and pamphlets concerning the professional career of John Smith, 1920-1940). The separation of the donor from his personal works, which figuratively represent his life blood, is tender, and having some formal record on hand helps bridge the gap between post partum and maturation of the collection. A sample receipt appears as Appendix 7-1.

DEED OF GIFT

Upon return to the library, the librarian writes an informal acknowledgment to confirm the gift, to outline any negotiations which transpired during the transfer, and to give some rough indication of how the collection will be handled in terms of time and organization. He reassures the donor of an independent appraisal, if the gift represents a possible tax deduction. The letter provides a continuing personal touch to alleviate the donor's concern for the security of his gift.

Accompanying the letter is a "deed of gift" which legally conveys the material from the donor to the library. Primarily, the library wishes full title and full control of all the gift. The deed should not commit the library unreasonably, and thus should avoid specifics, such as method of organization, type of access, and disposition of unwanted materials. The deed may state that the library possesses or will possess the literary or publication rights if the gift contains material of publishable quality.

Publication rights of an illustration, for example, often belong to the original publisher who purchased it to use as a frontispiece or dust jacket, even though the publisher later returned the illustration to the artist. Were the library or one of its users to attempt publication, it would be essential to know who owned the publication rights.

Similarly, a good set of architectural drawings of a building about to be resold or remodeled has a cash value. Unless the rights were transferred to the library, the architectural firm ought to benefit financially when another architect or real estate broker employs the plans to convert or promote the sale of the building. The new architect and potential buyer want to know about plumbing, heating, wiring, bearing walls—the plans are invaluable. Sample deeds of gift appear as Appendices 7-2 and 7-3.

The deed of gift is a legal instrument which transfers more than just paper to the library. It may spell out financial benefit from use or publication, or specify restricted use for a designated period, the briefer the better. Philosophically, the librarian ought to refuse gifts with restrictions regarding use; practically, those limitations are probably temporary, protecting the donor or his family from some embarrassment for a specified period of years. If the librarian does not accept such a restriction, the collection may well be destroyed as the donor broods upon the sensitive, personal nature of the files.

Maintaining a good donor relationship permits the librarian to keep current on the donor's status. Has a family death changed the situation? Does the donor's death terminate the restriction? A serious researcher, too, may wish to contact the donor to seek access to the collection; by stating background, purpose, and detailed plans, he may gain permission to use the restricted file.

PHYSICAL RECEIPT OF THE GIFT

As soon as the cartons arrive at the library, they need review. The librarian has some familiarity with the contents, and the more comments and assessments he makes quickly, the better. He may have shown restraint or tact at the donor's home in terms of expressing himself directly and effectively. Segments of the gift may have been wretched; others so superb that they more than balanced the poor material. He may have a rough outline in mind to transform the materials into a workable order, following a pattern established with an earlier collection, and he may know the appropriate employee to bring order to the collection.

RECORD OF RECEIPTS, REGISTER, GIFT IDENTIFICATION

Pertinent facts about the gift should be recorded. An example of our box label is given as Appendix 7-4. The label, affixed to each box, indicates the creator of the material; it states whether the gift is new or an addition or addendum to a previous gift; it suggests the person who will organize the material or the level of competency necessary to organize it. "Model" points out previous inventories upon which to base the new inventory; "remarks" include such things as a rough assessment of contents, donor restrictions, special materials for which to watch, or a suggestion for handling one segment.

When a library receives twenty or thirty such gifts a year and processes them within six months or a year, this system of carton management is satisfactory. Larger libraries and archives often employ a numerical sequence and store cartons accordingly, such as 78-0001, indicating that this is the first gift in 1978. After this identification number appears the individual box number as well as the total count within the series—6/22, the sixth box of a total of 22. With a larger program, a gift register or series of temporary working cards to identify the gifts serves as control. Kenneth Duckett's *Modern Manuscripts: A Practical Manual for Their Management, Care, and Use* provides a thorough review of accession registers.

The correspondence folder or travel diary has a record of the librarian's reactions, impressions, and recollections concerning the visits to the donor. These will refresh his memory and assist the future manuscript organizer. The donor's casual remarks about materials, loss by fire, changing file arrangements at different points in his career, or transfer to dead storage will help the organizer understand the complexities of the cartons. With working notes, a rough outline of contents as indicated on each box label, and the jottings made within each carton at the donor's home, the librarian has a fair control over what he is to sort and arrange.

SORTING AND ARRANGEMENT

The primary concern of the librarian is working with the manuscript gift, but seemingly unassociated books, journals, and pamphlets may directly relate to the material with which he is to work. Sorting out unwanted or irrelevant material ought to proceed in conjunction with or after the arrangement of the collection. We employ a form to record the progress of a manuscript gift, retaining the form with the creator's folder. The form appears as Appendix 7-5.

Organization of material, administrative management, and use of an archive is very different from that of an historical manuscript collection, the type most often maintained by a library. An archivist retains the existing order of files, generally institutional, association, governmental, or corporate records. He creates his finding aids, or inventories, from the files as they exist. An historical manuscripts librarian or curator may adopt this technique, if the file system is workable. More often, having received a personal collection with little or no order, he must create an arrangement that will facilitate use. The librarian thinks of his manuscripts as papers; the archivist considers his collections as records. Many publications exist on the arrangement and care of archives and historical manuscripts collections. The discussion that follows relates primarily to the librarian's function, not the archivist's.

Providing proper intelligent arrangement of a manuscript collection is vital, if none exists. As the librarian examines each carton seriously, he takes time to study, think, reflect, and postulate on how the collection might best be assembled to benefit the future user. The librarian has secured typed or handwritten materials generally giving a personal or administrative contemporaneous record of an event, period, life, or movement in the form of letters, article or book manuscripts, speeches, essays, diaries, journals, documents, and similar first-hand accounts. These records in themselves are sufficiently important to support serious use and study. A selection of inventories appears as Appendices 7-6, 7-7, and 7-8.

The librarian considers the organization in much the same fashion in which he would outline a simple theme or paper, with major points supported one by one with lesser records. To present the important aspects of the collection, he begins with the most important materials, diaries or journals, followed by correspondence files. He may then select working manuscripts of books, articles, or speeches; then supporting subject or research files for completed or incomplete projects; and finally the least important or associated materials. Professionally, as explained in other texts, he might consider groups, sub-groups, series, and sub-series.

Four things occur almost simultaneously as the librarian works. First, he establishes what he hopes to be a final, logical order. Second, he discovers that he may become vicariously involved with the creator, with his passions, failures, triumphs, or devotion to a cause. Third, he begins to wonder where missing records are: how did a particular event turn out? His questions and concerns are not unlike those of the future user, and thus he makes note of all those questions. He may return to the donor to seek the answers, to locate the missing material, and to find supporting documents in other collections known to the donor. Fourth, he sets aside those things which appear completely extraneous to the collection—items which might benefit other sections of the library or could be returned to the donor or be destroyed as worthless.

ARRANGEMENT TECHNIQUES

The librarian works with two basic arrangement systems—alphabetical and chronological. He utilizes cataloging and indexing techniques for personal and corporate entries. Occasionally, an individual's collection will become, in reality, the records of an association, and the collection should then be considered as the formal files of the corporate group, with an added entry given to the individual, without whose interest the files would have been lost. In most cases, files are obviously personal or corporate and are donated under one basis or the other. We have referred to "donor" and considered him synonymous to "creator"; in reality, the creator's files may have been donated by his widow, daughter-in-law, or business associates, but the manuscript collection is maintained under the creator's name, the user's proper approach to the collection.

In addition to the obvious manuscript materials, such as letters and diaries, other items associated with the career or event, including posters and handbills (often called broadsides), tapes, videotapes, recordings, transcriptions, and pamphlets, should be retained and described as part of the collection. If these items have more immediate or potential use within another area of the library, they should be carefully described and identified before removal from the collection proper.

Correspondence is the most common section of each gift and frequently the most important. If there is a workable arrangement, it should be retained. Unfortunately, most creative people do not maintain organized files. The librarian must bring order to chaos.

Letters sent, or "outgoing letters," are generally in the form of carbons or drafts written by the individual to others. When put into chronological order, they provide a running autobiographical account. An alphabetical arrangement of the incoming correspondence, letters received by the donor, provides an index to all the names in the collection and enables the user to find quickly whether another specialist has corresponded with the subject, when, and how often. The user can correlate the letter received with a reply, simply by checking the list of letters sent by date.

Here again, the librarian needs to establish personal and corporate entries. Incoming correspondence written on business, corporate, foundation, or association letterhead may be of either a personal or business nature. Whether the entry is personal (under the writer's name) or corporate (under the business), the provision of the alternative name within parentheses better informs the user.

Other texts provide far more detail on the mechanics of manuscript collection maintenance. Files should be stored in acid-free folders, generally no more than 1/4" thickness to each folder; the folders ought to be placed in proper archival boxes, also acid-free, and the boxes should be stored in a controlled access area with relatively constant temperature and humidity.

Each unidentified item ought to be identified with a soft pencil notation indicating author, date, source, working title, or the like. This is especially true with a collection of undated letters still in envelopes and signed with first name only. Postmarks and return addresses may provide the needed information.

Each collection should be maintained as a separate unit under the creator's name. A collection should be kept to benefit present and future users; it is not a memorial to the donor, to be kept and arranged as he wishes.

Many collections are transferred to the library over a span of years during which there may be three or four duplications of the same file system. When no further gifts are expected, a single file system should be created within the organized pattern.

Paper clips, staples, rubber bands, high-acid clippings, and transparent tape are all enemies of paper and, thus, of manuscripts. These should be removed to assure as long a life of the material as possible.

THE MANUSCRIPT INVENTORY

Retrieval of information is the rationale for creation of a logical order. A collection that has refined order but that lacks descriptive access is almost useless. The user should not need to examine everything if he is seeking several short answers, nor should he be given uncontrolled access to the files. The inventory saves wear and tear on the collection and provides better access and good reference service, while allowing the scholar to use his time with the collection efficiently.

The good descriptive inventory facilitates preparation of the detailed catalog card, which may be used for a manuscript catalog or to report a collection for submission to *The National Union Catalog of Manuscript Collections*, published by the Library of Congress. The donor, too, is impressed by receipt of the cards and is enraptured by the inventory. That inventory will serve later as an example of the care and efficiency with which the library handles its collections; it is an excellent publication to offer a prospective donor.

INTRODUCTION TO THE INVENTORY

The librarian can offer some editorial judgments when he writes an introductory statement to the inventory. He may provide further elaboration: a major segment of the collection was destroyed by a house fire; a series of letters recounts an historical event; letters from a relative shed much light on the problems and responsibilities borne by the creator; or a major move from the East to the West Coast during World War II accounts for the lack of files before 1944. The librarian can assess the research potentials of the collection, in positive and negative senses, indicating strengths, weaknesses, gaps, and hidden resource potentials.

TRANSMITTAL OF THE INVENTORY TO THE DONOR

When sending the inventory and introduction to the donor, the librarian should solicit his assistance in making corrections; working from holograph manuscripts allows many chances for error in names, titles, and dates. The donor can also provide further biographical detail needed to make the introduction or formal cataloging complete. The donor is generally willing to respond to the library's form, of which we include a sample as Appendix 7-9. The response supplies missing biographical data and may reaffirm the intelligent guesses based on the manuscripts the librarian had at hand. Identifying the inventory as "Preliminary Inventory" allows the donor an opportunity to make proper changes and gives a future librarian flexibility to alter the original organization.

The librarian can pose questions that arose as he examined the collection. It is important to have the donor's written response so that the future user will know what disposition was made of missing parts. The donor, too, may be willing to help with the pile of miscellaneous manuscript fragments and single letters signed with a first name only.

Few collections are ever complete. The donor will discover and offer more material. In turn, additions to the collection may come from other family members, associates, or friends, and each increases the value of the original donation.

DISCARD

Segments of the gift may not relate to the manuscript collection. While the donor has some idea of plans for disposal, he should not need an accounting of each decision. As mentioned earlier, the librarian has several choices: returning unwanted material to the donor; passing it along to other sections of the library, to other libraries or appropriate institutions, or to a dealer; or destroying it.

Certain obvious materials—bank statements, wills, deeds, insurance policies—are probably important to the donor, and they may well have been included in the gift by mistake. However, returning papers to the donor simply because of their lack of importance to the library may provoke questions; the donor wants a rationale for the decision on each and every piece. It is better to secure initial permission to destroy unwanted material than to return a few items.

Placing material elsewhere within the library benefits the entire library. Marginal material, too good to throw away and yet not quite appropriate for the collection, can be used in vertical files, as duplicate copies of popular books or standard reference sets, or to fill in a gap in a magazine file. A careful record must be kept for the donor's file. Books and periodicals not written by or about the creator are seldom retained with the manuscript collection.

Dispersal of unwanted material to other libraries, institutions, or dealers must be conducted carefully. Does the library have the right to dispose of the material in this manner? Does the other institution or dealer wish the material, or is the librarian assuaging his conscience by shifting the responsibility for disposal to someone else? Book drives or foreign libraries ought to receive the same consideration; neither are dumping grounds for unwanted, hopeless material. Sale or exchange with a dealer provides an excellent outlet for good material. The more sincere the relationship with the dealer, the more he will respond with quality exchanges and good leads. The librarian must be sure to avoid any charges of collusion; he may wish to offer material on a bid basis.

Because of the personal nature of manuscript discards, some care should be given to what goes into the trash, where papers, bills, and canceled checks are available for inspection. Many stamp or cover collectors, amateur book-men, and book scouts enjoy prowling; the librarian would not want someone to ask the donor about further envelopes or magazines, mentioning all those items he had found in the library's trash. There is already much negative publicity about school libraries burning or destroying books; pulping un-wanted books and manuscripts is a necessity, but it should be done with discretion.

APPRAISALS

Tax deductions are among the major motivations for donations to educational institutions, and the librarian must be aware of the present tax situation. The most obvious tax benefit is that derived from the gift of a book or books, something nearly as tangible as the cash given to a charitable foundation or a church. Less obvious and far more complex is the determi-nation of the value of manuscript gifts.

Much of what has been written on appraisals has been lofty in philos-ophy and not too practical. Neither the librarian nor the donor can appraise the gift. Both are interested parties in the appraisal: the donor because he wants a high figure, the librarian because he wants to secure the collection. Neither has adequate expertise, knowledge of buying and selling manuscripts, or familiarity with fair market value (the price established between a willing seller and a willing buyer).

Some librarians have arranged with other libraries to do appraisals for one another, but such collusion is obvious and illegal. Others have sought advice from the local second-hand bookman, whose knowledge of the manu-script market is nil, but whose courage in appraising manuscripts is incredible. His appraisal figure is often low, perhaps with some realization that his figure and services are negligible when examined by the Internal Revenue Service. The antique dealer, the estate appraiser, and even the real estate appraiser prepare manuscript evaluations, but their statements have little validity.

An appraiser whose competence falls within the realm of the donor's gift is necessary. A specialist, with a sound reputation for buying and selling at market prices, knows his field. The donor receives two formal documents:

the appraisal and the statement of the appraiser's qualifications. The appraiser has solid figures to substantiate his position, should the Internal Revenue Service question him or the appraisal become a court case. The donor files the appraisal statement, the appraiser's supporting statement, and a copy of the library's inventory of the gift with his tax return.

Many institutions claim publicly that the donor pays the appraiser's fee. In reality, if the collection is sought by the library, the library should pay the appraiser's fee, which will be far lower than the collection would have cost if the donor had placed it for sale on the open market. For the appraiser's fee, the librarian has secured the appraiser's expertise and a legal document to support the donor's claim for tax relief. The libraries that have complained loudest about the donor's responsibility to pay for an appraisal are the libraries that lament the loss of collections to other institutions.

The appraiser needs to be familiar with the library's collection and program. Communication is important; if the librarian is aware of appraisals of similar material, he should share the information with the appraiser. The appraiser, too, is likely to refer collections to the librarian.

Richard Nixon signed into law the Tax Reform Act of 1969, which stated that the creative person—artist, writer, or attorney—was no longer able to donate his own papers at their fair market value. The creative person could donate his work, but could deduct only the value of the materials used in its creation—paper, pencil, ink, typewriter ribbon. Several attempts to restore at least a portion of the tax advantage have failed in Congress. Developments concerning Nixon and the backdating of his manuscript gifts to pre-date the 1969 tax law have done considerable damage to the cause of restoring the former tax incentive.

I.R.S. has taken another serious step affecting the same creative donors. While the creative person's files are worth only paper and ink should he wish to donate them during his lifetime, those same papers have a fair market value the moment he is dead. If he has made no provision in his will to give them to an educational institution, his estate skyrockets in value because of the formerly worthless papers. The individual is forced to make a provision in his will or destroy his papers during his lifetime, if he is to spare his heirs taxes much larger than anticipated just a few years ago.

Chapter 8

MAINTAINING DONOR INTEREST

Proper care and feeding may provoke the donor to make further contributions, to suggest and/or pursue leads, and to talk with others about his treatment by the library. By writing once or twice a year and by mailing the library periodical or keepsake, the librarian keeps in touch with his contributor—learning about his health, current location, future plans, and family news. Maintaining current files encourages more gifts and support and occasionally assists users of the donations.

CONTINUING DONOR CONTACT

Library publications remind the donor of the library and his special stake in the institution. Our library issues a periodical twice yearly which contains two or three articles based on manuscript gifts and includes news notes about other recent donations. It provokes appreciative acknowledgment from a good many donors or potential donors. The semi-annual mailing keeps us abreast of address and name changes, as the postal service supplies them. A keepsake need not be issued by the library but may simply be a good collection of regional poems, an etching of a literary figure, or a copy of an historic broadside, received as duplicates in a large gift. On the other hand, a keepsake issued by the library may feature one of its recent acquisitions, a letter, poster, photograph, or document.

The librarian is in a unique position to supply reference service to his contributors. He sends reviews of the donor's book or of other books of interest, newspaper clippings, or citations to journals or books. The reference department has the current addresses of friends with whom the donor has lost contact. The benefactor knows that "his" library is aware of his special concerns.

As he writes on behalf of the library, the librarian includes news stories or press releases about the gift or about similar gifts which the original donation provoked. He may talk about use and users of the collection. He can seek letters from administrative officers to express formal appreciation, provided the acknowledgments are well written, expressing some specific knowledge of the contribution, and not simply a public relations effort from the public relations department officer. The librarian should avoid provoking administrative form letters that do not mention the donor's unique materials or that place the donor's name in routine institutional solicitation programs, resulting in a tasteless series of letters or telephone calls asking for $5 cash contributions. The librarian's relationship with his executive officer should be close, so that he can depend on a meeting or dinner between donor and chief.

The librarian might write about some incident that has amused him as he arranged the collection or might use the nickname that the donor's friends use regularly. Even a greeting card for a holiday or birthday is appropriate, and its brief message may convey as much as a long, formal letter. How much easier it is to write "planning to pick up those files soon" than to create a long formal letter, indicating the librarian's willingness to make another trip to secure additional files.

That return personal visit is necessary, if, when the major gift was consummated, the donor still wished to retain certain records. Being too forceful in seeking everything at one time may mean loss of the entire gift. The librarian may be unable to convince the donor that dust and dirt mean nothing, or that the librarian is ready to crawl through the basement or attic for the remaining material. The good housekeeper is sometimes so concerned about the status of his home that he will not allow the librarian access to that dark corner of the cellar. The personal letter is written to gain access to the dark corner, for without that material, the collection is incomplete.

An evening meal or cocktails with a good donor develops an advantageous social relationship. The librarian ought to record in his notebook the donor's suggestions of leads, names, addresses, and specialties. That notebook is essential while traveling; six or seven such meetings each day lead to a very confused memory and a hopeless jumble. We are more than pleased when the donor produces his address book with properly spelled names and correct addresses. Having this data aids tremendously in researching and preparing a letter to the next potential donor. Such a meeting may, on the other hand, provide a repetition of information already extant in the collection or even a senile account of something about which the librarian now knows more than the donor's fading memory can recall. In that case, because the librarian's travel time is limited, further visits should not be planned.

The researcher may be helpful in donor relations, if he has already carefully examined the gift; his genuine interest and intelligent questions please the donor. However, permitting the user to visit the donor with the hope that the donor will do the research for him is a mistake. If he does not know as much as possible about the subject's career before making a personal visit, the encounter is a poor reflection upon the library and its users.

Most libraries have meetings of friends, boards, or associates, and at such a time, it might be appropriate to invite the donor for special recognition. Articulate donors might be asked to speak on their specialties or simply to present their collections formally to the library. Donors who live too close to the library, however, may become regular guests at all meetings, ready to take more than their share of the limelight or to haunt the library to guarantee that their gifts receive deserved attention, care, and love.

PRESS RELEASES, PUBLIC RELATIONS

Unless the gift has outstanding significance, preparation of a press release upon receipt of the gift is usually premature, for the librarian is not yet familiar with the unorganized cartons. At that point, the interested viewer or user would be dismayed to see the disarray or to learn that the materials will be unavailable for six months or a year. When the collection is arranged and on the shelf, the release should be prepared, often based on a careful editing of the introduction to the inventory. The story should be sent to the local press, the newspaper in the donor's city, the appropriate professional journals, and the proper library and archival publications, such as *American Archivist, American Libraries,* or *Wilson Library Bulletin.*

Radio appearances or speeches to clubs, professional associations, societies of bibliophiles, friends of the library, and groups of researchers evoke interest in the new acquisitions and provoke thoughts among the audience of similar potential contributions. Using a recent gift as a point of departure for a talk or article allows the librarian to present an explanation of what and why he solicits in a special area. Television presents a visual opportunity to publicize the library's most attractive recent gifts and affords the librarian another chance to talk about his collecting program.

CORRESPONDENCE FILES

An efficient filing system is essential in order to maintain good records and effective donor relations. The key file is the correspondence file, arranged by the manuscript creator's name. In addition to solicitation letters and responses, each contains memoranda, working notes made as the librarian organizes the collection, a copy of the gift receipt, a deed of gift, the full inventory with occasional private notations for use of the staff, financial appraisals, requests for use, biographical material about the creator and/or donor, press releases, and a local map to pinpoint the donor. We have sometimes divided this material into two or three folders containing the correspondence, legal papers, and inventories. Infrequently, the donor becomes more important than the three or four collections he has donated, and the files are transferred to the donor's name, rather than the creator's. Another librarian at a much later date ought to be able to reconstruct the whole gift negotiation from the file, and he will expect sufficient information for finding the heirs of the donor.

NAME CARD FILES

The name file should contain on cards all the names with which the librarian has dealt, favorably or unfavorably. It should include names of everyone to whom a letter has been sent, whether creator, creator's widow, married daughter, executor, brother-in-law, secretary, or associate, along with, for corporate subjects, the corporate name and those with whom the librarian has corresponded or met. Many married daughters write without mentioning father's name; many families will have two or three interesting manuscript creators, and the librarian may avoid writing to the same person two or three times, each time about a different possible gift. The card, appearing as Appendix 8-1, first gives the individual's name, and then a reference to the entry under which the correspondence file is or was established, as well as a geographical location, which refers to the second card file.

GEOGRAPHICAL CARD FILES

The geographical file helps the librarian plan his travel time efficiently. When he is making a trip to a city fifty or more miles away, he could meet half a dozen potential donors on one trip, if a geographical file locates all possible donors in one town or in several neighboring towns. Our geographical cards are arranged first by state, then by city, and finally alphabetically by creator. Each card is the "lead card" from which the "name file" is created, the typist secures information, and the librarian retrieves biographical data. A sample card appears as Appendix 8-2. The notes in the lower section of the card indicate suggested biographical or reference sources.

The geographical file might also contain an information card for each city in which several donors reside. The card could contain names, addresses, and telephone numbers of carton suppliers, shippers, or former donors who now will occasionally do a chore for the library, as well as restaurants, motels, and book stores.

DEAD CARD FILES

Geographical or lead cards that are no longer active are removed to a "dead" or inactive file. The card records with a brief notation some negative result or decision that resulted in its removal from active status:

1. The potential donor has written that he has placed his files elsewhere, never retained files, destroyed them, or sold them.

2. The librarian has met the prospective donor and learned personally that one of the above is true.

3. The postal service has returned the librarian's letter or letters with a notation that precludes further effort without a better address.

4. The creator and/or his heirs have not been located either through the library's own resources or through contact with associates or friends.

5. The librarian's research has found that the creative person died without heirs, or if there were heirs, they died without issue.

The negative information in the "dead" files provides a good idea about where collections have been placed, or what areas of a state or region seem to have effective collecting programs. A pattern may indicate that another library is collecting a particular subject, although not reporting its holdings to *The National Union Catalog of Manuscript Collections*, or that alumni gifts to an institution without adequate manuscript facilities and staff are never reported.

OTHER FILES

A "come-up," "tickler," or reminder file includes potential donors who were sent first letters and who will need a reminder letter within a specific period, if they do not respond. The file also records those potential donors who indicate that they will have some decision or a shipment to send on a specific date. The come-up file, then, indicates when to write to whom about what. See Appendix 8-3.

A personal travel diary or journal is very helpful to the librarian and to the library, especially when indexed by name. When visiting six or eight donors, seeing three or four collections, and packing five or twenty-five cartons, the librarian recalls a day of conversation, information, and work. The diary incorporates those details which enable the librarian to recall details of the gift, to respond to questions posed at the time of the gift, and to maintain a beneficial relationship with the donor. The diary recounts something of the personality of the contributor and his family, of the home and community, of the importance of the books and manuscripts, and of the donor's special interests and hobbies. It records some of the tragic or amusing personal incidents and small details that occur during field work, and by re-reading it, the librarian can refresh his memory about a specific donor and the donation. A subsequent letter or visit may mention the donor's favorite authors, antique furniture, passion for dogs or cats, as well as those materials and leads which had to be ignored on the last visit.

A series of cards with a description of each collection, name of donor, and value of the gift serves as the basis for an annual report or summary of the program. An extra card from the manuscript catalog might well be the basis of this report to the administrative officer, the library board, or the parent institution. The report is useful, too, in seeking additional support in staffing or funds.

COOPERATION AND COMPETITION
AMONG MANUSCRIPT COLLECTIONS

Much speculative, philosophical writing appears concerning cooperation among libraries, and the difference between theory and practice may have created the difference between poor and good manuscript collections.

To speak of cooperation first, our practice, when discovering a collection of no interest to us, is to contact an institution that might consider it of value; similarly, if the potential donor informs the librarian that he has already made provision in his will to bequeath the work to another institution, the soliciting librarian withdraws. If the major part of the donor's material is already preserved elsewhere, the librarian should withdraw and consider writing a tactful letter to the other institution, suggesting it might be appropriate now to secure the remaining files.

In terms of practical competition, the librarian who finds that another institution took a small portion of the collection some years before his own inquiry and did not seek further materials or maintain contact with its former donor can assume that the collection is his, almost by default. A library, such as the Presidential libraries, that seeks to secure only a segment of a personal collection leaves the creator with the impression that the remainder is worthless. Most often, the creative person's entire file is important, reflecting his growth, maturity, experience, diverging interests, and application of knowledge gained in one subject area to another. To solicit and secure materials concerning only one segment of the donor's career without suggesting that the remaining files are also important (even if not to the soliciting library) is a disservice to the donor and to all serious users of the research material. Many small gifts are consummated as the result of a single letter or visit, while the donor remains "stuck" with the major portion of his work. Similarly, the library that broadcasts a form letter appealing for anything at all—an object, book, manuscript, or autograph—hardly deserves consideration by those libraries which build research collections.

Extensive cooperation and microfilming among institutions with manuscript collections is generally urged by libraries with weak manuscript holdings. They wish to gather for their own collections all existing material in a subject area or geographical region from other libraries with established collections. The proposal may or may not offer more than the "centralization" of the materials.

Regional or subject cooperation, whereby libraries determine who will collect what and where, leaves the potential donor with no apparent decision in the matter, which is totally false. A library solicits manuscripts to support a need and demand for such records by its users; the deed of gift transfers ownership of the gift to that particular library; and the recipient of the donation has the professional obligation to organize, house, protect, and oversee use of the materials.

Loaning manuscripts, or microfilming or photocopying them to enable other libraries to enlarge their collections, violates the trust that the donor placed in the library. When documents are copied, neither the library nor the parent institution has control over their subsequent use. If the collection is misused—letters quoted out of context, a manuscript published without proper permission or credit, or sensitive material broadcast widely—it is the owning library that suffers, not the institution for whom the copy has been produced. The outcome might include a law suit, loss of existing donor confidence, and few opportunities to secure further donations.

More than enough material is available to collect for serious use and historical benefit. Libraries that complain that others have collected their specialties must consider why they have not been successful. Priorities should be reassessed to see what materials should be collected for future research.

Respect and cooperation among libraries can enhance the extent and value of manuscript collections for present and future users. A better record of historical endeavor results from careful selection and solicitation of potential donors.

Chapter 9

ILLUSTRATORS AND AUTHORS OF BOOKS FOR CHILDREN:
A Study of Collecting on a National Basis

A few years after the author of this text had been at the University of Oregon, we collected the personal letters, journals, sketches, dummies, and manuscripts of several successful Northwest illustrators and authors of books for young adults and children. At that time, our concern was to preserve the contemporary cultural and creative heritage of the Northwest. We realized that a number of talented, creative individuals with both regional and national importance in the children's field lived in the Northwest, and yet no library had sought to preserve their work.

I have chosen this particular topic as an example because of my first-hand knowledge of the entire collecting program, from selection of subjects to use of the collections. Having corresponded with and/or met 750 authors and illustrators, I am familiar with the types of materials that are saved by the creative individual, with the people who use such records once they are no longer important to the individual, and with other institutions that have collected or are collecting within the field.

When we realized that an area of creative endeavor was being largely neglected by libraries within this country and recognized the present and potential demands by graduate students and faculty for such unique materials,

we began to collect intensively. Only two libraries were noted for holdings
in the children's field—New York Public Library, for its strong resources in
published material, and Dr. Irvin Kerlan's collection, emphasizing prize-
winning books of both authors and illustrators.

Present and future use seemed obvious on an academically oriented
campus. To demonstrate the creativity of the artist and author, we sought
those records which were unique to the individual—sketches, roughs, story
outlines, synopses, drafts, notes, working files, and correspondence with
editors, agents, associates, friends, readers, and publishers. Our library school,
graphic arts students, creative writing faculty, journalism and history departments, and art school all had appropriate concerns for primary research
materials. In other words, users were present, and future use was equally
apparent.

Not only did we have active interest on campus, but we had the germ
of a good collection already in the Library: we had three or four basic collections, which had been gathered in the region and yet which had national
significance. The papers of Will Corbin and his wife, Eloise Jarvis McGraw,
were excellent; the files of Mary Jane Carr were in demand; the working
drawings, roughs, and finished illustrations of Pers Crowell were artistically
exciting; and the records of a husband-wife team from an earlier generation,
Arthur and Mary Mason, added to the geographical distribution of the collection, for their roots had been in New York.

While our book collection was oriented toward an instructional level, and
while secondary study could be conducted from secondary sources, we needed
basic source materials to conduct primary research which would lead to
national and international studies. We needed all those singular items, such
as letters, sketches, and dummies, which the creative individual used in practice and in theory in producing a unique genre, the twentieth century
American children's book. Should we, we asked, seek out only the authors
and illustrators, or should we be concerned with editors, publishers, printers,
reviewers, and literary or art agents?

Only in the artist's studio or the writer's office or workshop were such
private, personal records likely to exist, almost always in the creative person's
possession, or in the hands of his heirs. Libraries had accepted individual
manuscripts or illustrations offered in grateful appreciation by an author or
illustrator. In effect, the gift was simply a museum piece, to place under
glass in a display case or on the wall, or, more often, to file and forget; its
format did not conform to the bookshelves, to the card catalog, or to standard cataloging procedures. The serious researcher needed to travel to the
home of each person, or to forget the project based on original sources.

We were concerned that the program, once begun, would receive support necessary to maintain it. Did we have room in the stacks, acid-free storage files or cartons, staff to organize and service the gifts, funds to maintain the collections, and financial resources for further travel to secure new donations? Would we always have users? Were we collecting in an area which would lose popularity and interest as current research interests shifted? We were well aware of the many ethnic collections that were springing up across the country, based on an immediate enthusiasm and obligation to do the right thing, right now. Were we planning a similar collection, based on a new, rising wave of interest? Did we have but a blind faith that future funding would be granted and that users would swarm to the campus in search of prime materials? These were difficult questions to answer; almost all our responses were qualified but positive, and yet we worried as we observed in more recent years one after another ethnic or political archive close or reorganize in order to comply with financial exigencies. How many collections were funded for a period, first as a library, then as a museum, and finally as a cultural center? Was our direction and foundation solid? Our worries intensified when we viewed the withdrawal of federal and foundation funding toward the end of the 1960s. How could such collections continue an active program? Without these funds and the funds of this decade, housekeeping remained undone, books uncataloged, and manuscripts unorganized; and with these obligations unfulfilled, users were non-existent.

We defined our scope. We had a small, knowledgeable staff devoted to the field; we had motivation, but we had to develop guidelines that would allow flexibility and yet not overwhelm the program with too broad a scope, with a field program too expensive to secure donations, and with a staff too large to be realistic. We recognized that the "Golden Age" of children's literature had occurred in this country between the years 1930 and 1955, roughly coinciding with the domination of the field by the great women editors whose role and authority was undisputed in major American publishing houses. At that time in publishing, the children's department was money invested in sound stock; the editors were excellent brokers, the investments solid, and the returns excellent. We chose to collect intensively in this country, with primary emphasis on the Golden Age, and secondary emphasis on earlier publications and the spinoff resulting from the Golden Age. The goals were within reach—we were able to travel to meet potential donors and evaluate what they had saved; we had the users; we were equipped already with a small manuscripts division, though its emphasis was on other fields; we knew the types of material we sought; and we planned to assemble a working collection from each artist or illustrator rather than acquire individual souvenirs or memorabilia.

When we began our collecting, we were fortunate in having the tax laws that benfitted the donor. Prior to the Tax Reform Act of 1969, the creative person was able to donate his work to an educational institution and receive full tax credit for "fair market value"—that amount that a willing buyer would pay for the material if the seller were to offer it on the open market. Tax motivation provoked some gifts, but we were pleased to learn in this area (as distinct from a good many others) that more often the donor's motivation was to share his working processes with others who might benefit from study of the gift. The spirit of friendship, cooperation, and understanding is very strong among the leaders of this period and field.

We sought to document "the whole individual" and not simply that segment of his career which pertained to the children's field or a prize-winning book. Thus, we met novelists, confession story writers, painters, commercial artists, teachers, professional historians, and biographers, as well as illustrators or writers of books for young people. We wanted the individual's working files, indicating how he worked in many areas, how he approached his problems, how he solved a technical aspect of a manuscript or illustration, and what or how he felt when he completed the book or article. Personal papers showed the creative individual as a spouse, parent, child, friend, with family and personal concerns and interests in areas widely divergent from children's literature. Perhaps the writer had a bent for history, Chinese art, or a conservative cause. Ours was not an effort to collect prizes, paintings, or souvenirs; we wanted records that showed how the individual worked and lived.

We based our collecting on a major principle. As a state-supported university, we knew we could not ask funding to collect "children's literature"; the cry from the taxpayers would be loud and proper, for state funds were needed for far more basic materials. We had to seek all materials as donations. To pay one individual and to beg materials from another would pit one artist against another and damage our own program. One regional author was distressed to find that three of her friends had received larger tax deductions than had she. She demanded the return of her files, which were impoverished in terms of solid research records, accounting for the low evaluation. We had yet to catalog the files, though they had been organized, and we returned them. Thus, even an appraisal can become a delicate, sensitive question.

In conceiving an effective collection program, we expected to create a snowball effect. The donors whom we contacted would continue to give during their productive lives, and we might expect to receive the residue upon their demise. Other authors and illustrators interested in presenting their materials to the University would, and did, write to us; friends and associates, as well as users, would, and did, inform us of other collections we might secure. In one surprising way, we ignored the fact that we did not have static collections; we did not leave room for the collections to grow when arranging them on the shelves.

In establishing the need to collect, we also examined the "right to collect." We were representatives of a respected educational institution with appropriate facilities, users, and space; we were not a shoestring operation, seeking to create something from nothing with continued pleas for support of any nature. While such a goal is admirable, it often leads to unwanted gifts of overwhelming size. Geographically, we were removed from the commercial publishing center of the country, but we had an active interest that had previously been exhibited by those who collected only books, notable manuscripts, or souvenirs. Ours was a new concept, at least in the field of children's literature. While exhibition of materials was a secondary purpose, ours was to be a collection based on recording the creative efforts of respected authors and illustrators of books for young adults and children.

Acceptance of memorabilia as part of a gift was dependent on the basic gift. Was the substantive donation the cake, with its memorabilia to be the frosting? Were the primary elements included in the gift—correspondence and working records, documenting the creative subject's efforts? If these were the core of the gift, the frills enhanced its attractive nature; otherwise, we did not wish the frills. Dolls, medals, certificates, awards, fan letters, commendations, or models meant nothing without the primary materials which led to the author's recognition. A useful author's collection had to have his correspondence with other authors, literary agents, editors, publishers, friends, associates, and readers, as well as his journals, notes, synopses, outlines, dummies, and manuscripts per se. We asked the artist for his working records—sketches, roughs, sketchbooks, story boards, dummies, final art, proofs, and correspondence of the same nature as the author's.

Selection of potential donors was an exciting process, for we had input from our staff, faculty, users, and those whose collections were already part of the Library. The professional and personal input was welcome, for, in addition to simple suggestions, we often had some private bits of information about the subject or a personal admiration for his work. Names also came from more basic sources, reading biographical materials in conjunction with suggestions that lacked good background information. We ignored the individual who seemed to be associated with an institution that might logically have an interest in his work—a school, library, museum, or gallery. Similarly, we checked many names against Hamer and the *National Union Catalog of Manuscript Collections*.

Once we had decided upon which authors and illustrators to contact, we needed to work with our telephone and city directories, if we knew roughly where our possible donors lived. Otherwise, we checked biographical blurbs on dust jackets, or used *Something about the Author, Junior Book of Authors, Who's Who in American Art, Who's Who in America* (and its regional volumes), and to a lesser extent, *Biography Index, The New York Times Obituary Index, Book Review Index, Horn Book, Contemporary Authors, Books Are by People,* and *School Library Journal.* At times, we wondered about the use of a biographical file taken from dust jackets and newspaper items; we were grateful when we learned how useful such a record could be to locate our subjects. Even the author's date or dates in the card catalog or *Children's Catalog* helped.

We arranged a card system, much as described in Chapter 8—one set arranged geographically and then by name of subject, the other file by name of subject or name of contact or pseudonym to serve as a cross reference file to the geographical cards. The geographical card became the key card with whatever information we had attached to it, or following it; there we included biographical or bibliographical data or personal information, source of our original lead, date we first wrote, collections in our possession of interest to the subject, special things about the donor of interest to us (notes on his technique, medium, specialty), phone number, names of spouse and children, age or death date, heirs, and our holdings of his work.

The subject was then written a rather personal letter stressing the Library's holdings, intentions, users, and general philosophy. Specifically, we indicated what we sought in terms of correspondence and associated materials. Modification had to be made in special situations. Any librarian who considers a similar project ought to work out his own letter and not broadcast a form letter appealing for any type of material. If the letter is an appeal for any and all materials, then the response is much the same, and the recipient becomes a trash disposal site, with a responsibility to retain the trash.

As we wrote the letters, we considered the subject's age, and thus we urged a gift at the moment, or at a future date, depending on the subject's need for his files. The elderly artist or author might have little need for old files, while the young, creative individual may be too young yet to decide what is of use. In the latter situation, it was best to ask the younger subject for his old correspondence, illustrations for earlier books, old working files, and dummies of published books, if they were not of use to him.

Responses varied, with refusals based on the present tax law, destruction or loss of the material, anticipation of future use, allegiance to another institution, or confusion as to what our letter sought. A response that indicated any sort of interest was considered seriously, and we attempted to arrange a meeting to answer the potential donor's questions and examine the materials in his possession. Among answers which we took to be positive were, in addition to the donor who understood and accepted our request, the person who dwelt upon the wrong materials (we assumed he had saved the proper things as well), the individual who suggested that others had better files than his (modesty was common among writers and illustrators of children's books), and even the "don't call us, we'll call you" variety. For the last subject, we waited several months and then rephrased our suggestion.

The card files continued to be useful as we gained information, even though the information was negative, for we recorded who had suffered loss by fire or flood; whose child lost the material at show-and-tell; which author destroyed files as he finished each book; what other libraries had received the individual's files. While we wish we could publish these results, we assume that a good many creative people would not wish the world at large to know of their losses.

If the initial letter did not provoke a response, we wrote a second one. The individual who ignored our first letter because he did not wish to deal with us was in the small minority. Most responses to the second letter were as favorable as those to the first. If the second letter was based on some new point of reference or interest, it provided us with a better letter and a different approach. Often response to the second letter indicated that the first was never received, and a good file system was necessary for us to provide a copy of our original letter. We wrote our second letter independently of the first, so that the recipient knew what we wrote without need to refer to any previous correspondence.

The response indicated confusion at times, and the fault often was that we had not expressed ourselves clearly. We rephrased and amplified what we said, or changed the thought completely, so that the recipient had another chance to consider our request. Occasionally, the individual we wrote was well advanced in years, and the problem was one of senility rather than of the phrasing of our letter.

We assessed our letters regularly to see whether we were achieving what we had planned. Were we reaching the potential donors? What were they telling us about their materials, our letters, and/or other libraries seeking similar work? We realized that we were conducting a proper program, that about 75 percent of those to whom we had written responded either to the first or second letter, and that all responses were important. We did not retain negative responses, but we did record the response briefly on the subject's geographical card, an approach that kept our correspondence files from growing.

In our responses to potential donors whom we had not met, we tried to be clear and direct, seeking to answer specific questions and then requesting a meeting if at all possible at the home, office, or studio of the subject. Field work, travel to meet donors, was an attempt to see the author, illustrator, or heir in the home, office, or studio where the potential donor was comfortable and where he kept his working files. The meeting allowed us to evaluate the donor, his age, health, situation, and family. Were we being unfair by taking something extremely precious to an elderly soul who needed to hold onto this last bit of substance to justify his existence in this world, or by seeking something of obvious value which ought to bring ready cash to the impoverished writer or artist? Did we need to act because of the donor's age, failing sight, soundness of mind, or a potential move? Did the unappreciative surviving spouse or child wish to get rid of all that clutter assembled by the creative individual?

In addition, the chance to view the material as it was originally housed and/or as it was saved was vital. One letter described "several tons" of files, which we consolidated into one carton; another spoke of "several cartons," which became two tons. Was the material intrinsically important? Was it still in condition to be saved and used? How was it arranged? The visit to James Daugherty was fascinating for he had kept everything, though he thought so little of its value that he had stored illustrations on the floor and even occasionally walked across them. Elmer and Berta Hader had carefully boxed, wrapped, and stored the working illustrations, three or four dummies, final drawings, manuscripts, and correspondence of each book as they completed it. Many of the visits, however, were fruitless, for we found that the artist or writer had destroyed files or that a flood, mice, or fire had done the process for him.

To see the material and to review its value in terms of the Library's interest helped us determine whether to pursue actively the possible donation. The on-site inspection also allowed the donor to meet us, realize our intentions were those expressed in the letter, and state more directly his thoughts about a possible gift. If the situation required more effort, we mustered our thoughts to support our stated interest.

Logistically, it was important to see the material and make a decision on how to pack, ship, and then receive it. What was the bulk? Was it too fragile to send by mail or truck? What was too large to be accommodated in standard book cartons or "mirror cartons" which the usual art portfolios fill quickly? To examine and assess the studio of Edward A. Wilson on Cape Cod was exciting, but to face the problem of shipping everything immediately was even more exciting. We carried a good many loads to a shack several miles away where the owner sold bait, ice, and acted as an REA (Railway Express) agent. The shipment for forty mirror cartons must have brought more business to the shed than REA normally saw in several weeks. It was best for us to make the moving decisions, and once accepted by the donor, to pack and move the gift ourselves.

Often we found that our examination led to a negative decision, and it was easier to talk with the donor and to tell him directly why we did not feel his collection was of value to our library. In evaluating a collection we almost always began to formulate in advance what we planned to say in declining the potential gift, giving thought to what alternatives could be found in disposing of the material.

The relationship established with the donor by visit was often a personal one, reflecting the interest of the Library and yet personified by its representative. The donor addressed his questions and comments to the librarian, and continued to do so after the visit, for he knew someone at the Library. His leads were almost always good, for between the correspondence and the librarian's visit, the donor had come to understand the Library's interests. Henry Pitz knew another illustrator whose studio was cluttered with art, and whose heirs did not know what decision to make about his illustrations; Pitz spoke on our behalf. On our part, we often asked about contemporaries, about the illustrator who added a fine touch to the writer-donor's books, or about the authors with whom the illustrator had worked. The donor-friend provided just the right information for us to approach someone who had been reputed to be unapproachable.*

The gift of a manuscript or art collection created by a children's illustrator or author entailed a series of professional responsibilities. How was the material to be organized and described? How was it to be preserved for both convenience and long life? By what means were users to be informed of its availability? The gifts had to be assembled, inventoried, preserved, and reported with dispatch; it was an obligation in exchange for the gift.

The author or illustrator lacked time, patience, inclination, and space to maintain orderly files. As his project was completed, he set aside whatever led to the final work, giving little attention to organizing or caring for what became "history"; the material was no longer useful or important to him.

We were to create order from each chaotic acquisition. A large gift entailed considerable examination, perhaps a preliminary sort, and then further reflection before establishing a system for logical arrangement. Did the collection relate to one book or many? Did it concern one aspect of the creative person's career? Did it include other interests, such as writing adult novels, illustrating magazine stories, abstract painting, or book reviewing? Did it

---

*The remainder of this chapter appeared in a somewhat different form as "Manuscript and Art Collections: Organization, Care and Use," in *Phaedrus, a Journal of Children's Literature Research*, 3, no. 2: 17-19 (Fall 1976).

contain unsold manuscripts or illustrations, or research for projects never brought to completion? What arrangement most easily satisfied questions posed by the future users? Did the Library already have a collection of a similar nature, with an arrangement to serve as model?

Necessarily, organization suited the individual collection. Working material for several books was generally arranged by book. The material for each title was divided into various components, progressing in order much as the book itself was created, from research notes and drafts to manuscript, galleys, and reviews, or from rough sketches, idea drawings, and dummies to the final illustrations and proofs. A count of manuscript pages or leaves, or measurements and graphic medium became a part of the description. Thus, working materials for one book appeared as:

Gramatky, Hardie

> Bolivar. New York, G. P. Putnam's Sons, 1961

>> Sketchbook. "Notes on Bolivar, 1960." Pencil sketches and text, notes, and outline. 316pp.

>> Dummy. "Next to final. Revised again September 1961." Pencil, ink, watercolor, gouache. 64pp.

>> Original art. Black and white unless otherwise noted. Ink, watercolor, gouache. 64pp.

>>> Jacket. 11 1/4 x 18. (9) 9 refers to number of versions
>>> End papers. 5 x 5. (1)
>>> Frontispiece. 8 1/2 x 10 1/2. (2)
>>> Title page. 8 1/2 x 10 1/2. (2)
>>> Pepito playing flute. p. 7. Photostat only.
>>> etc. etc. . . .
>>> [full description of every item is included in the actual inventory]

>> Galley proofs. 9pp.

>> Color and page charts. (2)

>> Book jacket proofs. (3)

>> Books: Bolivar. New York, G. P. Putnam's Sons, 1961. Bolivar. London, World's Work, 1962. d.j.

Some collections were less book oriented, perhaps focusing upon biographical materials. We emphasized the content by arranging the acquisition from most important to least significant segments. Hence, diaries, journals, and sketch books appeared first, for they represented a candid, autobiographical account of the creative person. Similarly, correspondence files depicted rather frankly the work, opinions, and life of the illustrator or author. By alphabetizing all the letters received, we furnished the user with a full list of names, an index to the correspondence. By placing all outgoing carbons, drafts, and/or copies in a chronological order, we assembled a biographical account, generally second only to diaries or journals in research value.

If book material comprised a segment of the gift, it was described next, followed by lesser writing or illustrating projects, such as articles, short stories, magazine illustrations, and tear sheets. Another section included publicity, reviews, fan letters, and school-initiated requests for biographical information from "my favorite author/illustrator." All published biographical or autobiographical accounts, photographs, interviews, and memorabilia comprised the final segment.

An example of a large collection might include the major divisions as outlined:

McGraw, Eloise Jarvis

  Business correspondence.

    Outgoing. 1967-1973. 117 and enc.

    Incoming.

      Atheneum. (Margaret McElderry, Florence Sczesny) 1971-1973 and undated. 25.
      Curtis-Brown. (Marilyn Marlow, Elizabeth Nowat, Jere Knight) 1968-1971. 24 and enc.
      General incoming correspondence. 1962-1972 and undated. 1 folder. Arranged alphabetically.

Personal correspondence.

Outgoing. 1966-1973 and undated. 73.

Incoming.

Bracken, Peg. 1969-1972 and undated. 26
and enc.
Clewes, Dorothy. 1962-1967. 19. etc. etc.
General incoming correspondence. 1962-1973
and undated. 1 folder. Arranged alphabetically.

Manuscripts. Novels.

Cheyenne Indian novel. Unfinished.
Preliminary notes: customs, tools, names.
Holograph revisions.10pp.
Historical background notes. Holograph
revisions. 13pp. etc. etc.

Manuscripts. Articles.

The cure for halfwayitis. *The Writer*. 1969.
Holograph research notes. 7pp.
Outlines. Holograph revisions. 9pp.
First draft. Holograph revisions.10pp.
Final draft. Holograph revisions. 8pp.

Lectures, speeches, courses.

Portland State University. 1966. 1 folder
Lecture notes, assignments, evaluations,
student work, miscellaneous publicity.

Biographical.

2 scrapbooks, college yearbooks, high school
yearbooks, stories written during school
years, photographs, drawings. 2 folders

In such a manner, we created order. Immediate steps to prolong the
life of each gift included removal of paper clips, pins, staples, tape, and rubber bands, along with high-acid newspaper clippings; all are harmful to paper.
We opened and flattened letters, broadsides, posters, and art, because folding
and unfolding paper leads to deterioration at the folds.

We wanted each letter to contain the writer's name, location, and date. If the information was lacking, we supplied the data from the envelope, using a soft pencil for notations. Similarly, book illustrations and sketches were identified individually to facilitate return to the proper file after use for a display or by a researcher or publisher.

The inventory of the collection was prepared while organization was in process, or from the final arrangement. As the records were placed in new, acid-free folders and then into archive cartons, Hollinger boxes, or Solander cases, a check of the inventory was obligatory. We recorded what material, such as oversized illustrations or posters, was stored elsewhere. Manuscripts were most conveniently housed with similar collections, with the accompanying illustrations stored with art materials due to physical size.

The inventory provided the user with access to the collection and spared wear and tear on the files. The user works with those materials essential to his purpose, while the remaining material is unused and not worn by repeated casual viewing.

An introduction to every inventory emphasized strengths and weaknesses in the acquisition. The correspondence files may be meager, extant for a short period within a long, creative career; the rough sketches for a book may be far more successful than those which were published; an unpublished manuscript may contain first-class autobiographical details about the illustrator or author. We took the opportunity to express our thoughts concerning the value and use of the acquisition.

The introduction often was revised to become a press release, ready for distribution to potential users in the library's own publications, *Imprint: Oregon* and *The Call Number*, as well as serial publications on children's literature. Submission of a formal description, to be filled out on appropriate information sheets, to the *National Union Catalog of Manuscript Collections* provided another opportunity to announce to the international scholarly world the existence and extent of our special acquisitions.

From a simple beginning in the late 1950s, our library now possesses three hundred substantial collections, almost all able to support individual study or use in conjunction with one or several other collections. At one time we did not realize that the friendships and professional relationships in the field would allow us to bring together, both directly in the field and spiritually in the Library, individuals who had worked closely in years past, whose frustrations and successes were common, whose interests and acclaim perhaps caused the separation of paths. We have a unique collection that reflects the scope which we set for ourselves, a collection representing the Golden Age of children's literature in this country. The estimated value of the collection as it was received by donation ran to $1,500,000; today, with inflation and an increased interest in the children's field, the collection is almost priceless.

Chapter 10

THE MUNICIPAL MUSIC COLLECTION:
A Working Example of a Larger Municipal Library's Solicitation
Program

Few local institutions gather and preserve a record of community
cultural origins and development, nor do they take a major role in supporting
and documenting local social and intellectual activities. Although generally
obligated to satisfy and support interests of both present and future users,
the city library rarely has sufficient funds, space, staff, and supplies to collect, organize, house, and maintain an in-depth collection of regional history.
Few can support collections that emphasize all local arts—writing, theater,
music, painting, and sculpture; the library's resources are too small. Necessity
dictates that the library emphasize one or two such aspects of community
life, rather than sample and create a superficially representative collection
from the entire spectrum.

The music collection found in nearly all larger municipal libraries
includes tapes, recordings, published music and scores, and books and journals about music. Such libraries have generally set aside an area designated
as the Music Room, have a support staff, and often a special card catalog for
this collection. A user community of students, teachers, professional

musicians, choir directors, and others already exists. With the nucleus established, the librarian might well consider whether he should undertake to preserve his local musical heritage by building a substantive research collection.

Frequently, library board, staff, users, friends, and community at large may place prime emphasis on a special collection reflecting the city's musical heritage, perhaps with the hope that if the program is successful and if adequate funding becomes available, the library will collect and preserve other areas of the arts as well. The decision to emphasize musical arts may be based on historical circumstances. Perhaps music was the earliest and most enduring art form of the community; the city may have a national reputation due to the success of a local composer, performer, orchestra, or music publisher; or, perhaps, a core collection has already been donated by the local symphony or music society. The library may have chosen to develop a music collection after recognizing that the local art museum had collected extensively, that the historical society had preserved the local historical materials, but that no one had stepped forward to insure that the primary resources for research in music would be saved.

Many of the examples in this chapter will be drawn from the author's personal experiences in developing an historically oriented music research collection at the University of Oregon. The elements comprising our solicitation program and those for a large city library are similar—careful consideration of the feasibility and suggested limitations of the collection; identification and examination of the sources needed for planning and collecting intelligently; establishment of a coherent and well-defined collecting policy; development of leads to possible donors or materials; establishment of solicitation strategy; organization of materials (shown as sample inventories in the appendix); and means of continuing and promoting the music collection.

FEASIBILITY

For several reasons, we decided to collect music within the state, and, more specifically the city of Portland, which represented both historically and currently the focal point for music education and performance within the state. Portland has had an unusually rich musical heritage—the earliest publishing of sheet music on the West Coast was centered in Portland; many performers of regional and national reputation originated in Portland; touring companies performed there regularly; students flocked from the hinterlands to pursue musical education in Portland conservatories; and several small, distinguished musical journals and periodicals flourished on Portland presses. Little documentation of all this activity had been preserved. In the late 1950s, very few American libraries collected primary music source materials, let alone popular American sheet music, readily found in every older home with a roomy attic, music cabinet, or piano bench.

Having recognized the need to preserve this rapidly disappearing musical heritage, we surveyed our university school of music and history department and ascertained that we had students in music, history, theater, psychology, and sociology who were interested in many varied aspects of music. With an established group of users, a special collections department which already had a few music gifts, and assigned space to house the collection, we combined our own research with practical application in developing potential leads.

INFORMATION SOURCES

The librarian acquaints himself with the music field by intensive reading and research, and, at the same time, he makes notes of personal names and organizations whose files might have some research or educational value to the library. His reading of professional literature, such as MLA *Notes*, combines education and research. Each librarian has some conception of what future plans and direction his collection may take, but he does pose a good many questions. He examines the relationship of music to other community elements. He asks whether local orchestras used their own arrangements, created by local musicians, or whether they purchased stock (published) arrangements. He establishes the authenticity of the local music publisher— was the business based on reputable publishing, or was the business known for its vanity appeal, charming through magazine and mail-order advertising the would-be composer or lyricist into paying for publication of a composition that delighted its creator alone. He seeks out information about the local vocalist who became successful nationally through television, radio, recordings, tape, or sheet music. He takes careful note when his users seek information about this local musician who has gone elsewhere as a national star; does the library wish to house the papers and recordings of the performer?

As his mind opens to the myriad types of information and to the possibilities of collecting, the librarian has a practical approach. He attempts to be thorough, examining the author, title, and subject catalogs, seeking material written by or about the community's musicians. He studies the tracings on catalog cards to catch references to a local matter he might otherwise miss—an annual song contest, a touring company which had summered regularly in his community, or several unpublished manuscripts by or about a local composer or performer.

He consults the shelf list in the music classifications, especially if the library maintains a special collection of state and local materials. He reads every local pamphlet about music, noting contents—author, subject, acknowledgments, bibliography, sources, and publisher. At the moment, he is steeping himself in his subject, as well as bearing in mind names of individuals, groups, companies, or associations whose files may be of interest.

As he gains expertise, hc uses mug books and local histories to find further biographical material about his potential donors or creators of materials, and he uses the indices to locate references to music and musicians. Again, he examines the author's sources and acknowledgments critically. He reads any local periodical or newspaper with a section on music and checks the older national music journals to see whether his region or city submitted news notes to a geographical column.

The librarian visits neighboring libraries to examine subject catalogs, shelf lists, and reference facilities, and he studies the state library collection, as well as any large academic or private collection known to have good music holdings. He should compare the strength of his library with others. Are his plans still valid, or has another library already assembled an extensive collection?

No matter what the library or occasion, he may have the opportunity to inform himself about local feuds or rivalries, the rise and fall of ballet or vaudeville, an aborted project for an opera company, or the social hierarchy among professional groups. He may talk with old-timers, stage-door Johnnies, patrons of music, or retired librarians. Interviewing those with sound memories and a genuine interest in assisting, he assesses the subject's ability to provide leads or political or financial support. He enriches his knowledge, gaining familiarity with dates, names, performers, and the library's present holdings. Policy is being shaped.

ESTABLISHMENT OF THE SCOPE OF THE COLLECTION, OR COLLECTION POLICY

Many librarians known for manuscript collecting operate with no policy and thus are not hampered by deciding whether a good donation fits within the bounds of a collection statement. On the other hand, a written policy may provide a graceful means to avoid an unwanted gift that is offered to the library with considerable political or social pressure. For example, the library is embarrassed when a newspaper article carries word of the donation of the local symphony's scores and arrangements; superficially the gift sounds most interesting, but the librarian is well aware that the gift includes several tons of shopworn, published scores, now lacking parts and organization. The story may represent the librarian's first knowledge of this potential gift; the policy may provide a means of escape, if a local controversy is about to occur. The policy, in general, is written to include generalities and provide leeway in acceptance of gifts. One example appears as Appendix 10-1. The library needs room to expand its concept to new media or subjects, while protecting itself against the inferior or inappropriate gift.

However, it is far better for the soliciting librarian to anticipate the reasons for refusing a collection than to fall back on collection policy. With tact and imagination, he can suggest other means of disposition: can the material assist a practicing music teacher, be transferred to an active music group, or even be pulped, if the material has been damaged by fire, water, insects or rodents? The properly phrased refusal may gain the donor's respect, while falling back on the policy statement suggests that the library is just another bureaucratic agency, bent on spending the taxpayer's money while refusing a substantive gift.

The librarian defines the limits of his collection. Will it be restricted to music composed by the musician while he lived in the area? Does the library accept only manuscripts of recognized composers, shunning the self-published or unpublished local musician and thereby missing a potential Charles Ives? Does the library seek written manuscripts, recorded materials, scores, arrangements, transcriptions, photographs, tickets, programs, invoices, posters, scrapbooks, printed materials, correspondence, financial accounts, and publicity from composers, lyricists, performers, musicians, music stores, local impresarios, music associations, and performing groups? What are the library's limits?

The librarian informs himself in matters of current laws and legislation on copyright, use, and performance. Is the collection to be available for all uses, including commercial? Who owns what rights upon donation of a collection of unpublished songs or of privately recorded tapes of a recognized performer? Can an orchestra or professional musician use at no cost the scores and arrangements created by a local musician? Who is to profit from financial aspects of the collection—performance, reproduction, or publication? Should the collection exclude commercial use and be limited to "serious" research?

Has the librarian emphasized only "serious" music to the exclusion of the folk singer, rock group, dance band, and advertising agency? Even the ad agency has produced radio and television jingles for commercial businesses, political campaigns, and socially oriented issues.

Should the librarian meet the composer who has fled from a larger city to reside in the librarian's city, or should he await the musician's appearance to offer his work to the institution? The library's policy may not indicate anything about such an attractive transplant, or may even have been written so narrowly that it restrains the enterprising librarian.

The librarian who is building a music collection has many questions to ask of himself and others in formulating a policy. In his desire to provide both broad coverage and narrow exclusions, he may forget the donor's interests, too. The collection policy ought to discuss what the donor can expect in terms of the library's plans, program, and obligations for maintenance, supervision, use, protection, and/or disposition of the gift.

LEADS

Earlier, we have spoken of the librarian's immediate need to inform himself about music and musicians, and, in that education process, to record potential leads. A card system is the most practical means of record-keeping: what and who have been considered and then located; what and who have been approached, and what response was secured. A system of cross references associates the orchestra with the donor of its materials, or the married granddaughter with the composer's manuscripts. The card system described in Chapter 8 is useful, though a geographical arrangement is unnecessary. All names ought to be arranged alphabetically into two alphabets—one with active leads, the other with inactive, discarded, incomplete, or hopeless subjects. Files become important as the collection grows and the librarian has a new reference to something he may possibly have researched before; his files provide a quick answer.

Local, regional, or national biographical dictionaries of musicians (some volumes are vanity, some commercial in nature) provide names and often addresses. Older volumes indicate the names of earlier important musicians, and comparison between an old and new volume will indicate who is still active. Those omitted may be inactive or deceased, and possibly their work may be more readily available and interesting than the active musician's files. Evaluation of such leads is important; the librarian might wish to check a second authority if he is unfamiliar with the musician, especially if the listing is in a vanity volume.

We have already spoken of the shelf list and of the components of the card catalog—sources of composers, lyricists, publishers, and occasionally, the cover artist. Recital programs, music club rosters, and music teacher association directories all provide names, and the librarian evaluates members or performers by reviews, reputations, and frequency of appearance. He then decides whether to take further action. The library's clipping file in the Music Room may contain biographies of performers or composers, articles on music-oriented associations, and histories of performing companies. Even the library's own correspondence concerning use of the collection and musicians who have performed within the building are sources of leads. While most music groups, trios, quartets, bands, choral societies, and similar organizations have records, the challenge is to find the person who possesses them; reading accounts or rosters may establish the senior member of each group, a starting point in the quest for older files. Records may be stored by default by the interested board member, supporter, or principal patron of the group. The performance or meeting hall may even have storage space in an attic, basement, or closet.

The local music hall manager, booking agent, or impresario has records, often of touring companies; backstage workers (the community musicians who were in the pit for opera, theater, or ballet) may have materials. In the same pit, or on stage, the theater organist and silent movie pianist enchanted the audience of another era.

Whenever the subject cannot be found in a current telephone directory, the librarian's general reference techniques are called into play. Will an older city directory provide a clue, furnishing the widow's first name, the same first name possessed by the present occupant of the home? Both the old and new city directory can help to establish this sort of information. Does the newspaper index contain any reference to the subject, his spouse, children, or associates, to whom the library can turn for current information? Does the library's own circulation files indicate that the subject or a member of the family is a borrower? When does the subject drop from a series of older telephone directories, and would it be possible to write the current occupant of the subject's old address, if that occupant has resided at the subject's home for some years?

DONORS AND MATERIALS: A PERSONAL VIEW

As we mentioned at the beginning of the chapter, we began our music collecting in Portland, Oregon. We had done considerable research and had written to potential donors or sought information regarding possession of possible gifts. Having used many of the suggestions made above as the basis to develop gifts, we speak from practical experience of the donor and the types of material we found he possessed. We attempt to explain why certain materials have proved interesting.

It was a delight to find among the files of a Portland piano teacher the letters which she had written as a young girl to her mother. She had come to Portland about 1915 to enter a local conservatory of music, while her mother remained at the wheat farm, several hundred miles on the far side of the Cascade range. The letters are full of a young lady's reaction to teachers, courses, and musical life of the community. Another collection of letters was in possession of a voice teacher. Her Prohibitionist mother had pressed her father to sell his hop farm, and with the tangible assets of the sale, her father had sent her and her sister from a small Oregon town to Berlin and then to Paris for two years of music education abroad. The letters written by the sisters to their parents contain fresh, untutored impressions, reactions, and criticism of noted European teachers and musicians. In their youthful innocence, they slept comfortably in Paris, armed with hatpins to fend off the lusty Frenchmen.

Emphasis upon education of the musician, composer, or performer led us in another direction. We discovered the files of several old conservatories in Portland. One school had been established in Salt Lake City at the turn of the century, but in the early 1920s its head moved to Portland, where he began a new institution. His widow still possessed the school's catalogs, programs, correspondence, student rosters, and other normal education materials. As an adjunct to his business as impresario, another Portlander had formed a music school, and we found that his nephew and widow had split what records survived from his turn-of-the-century venture. Again, we were almost able to reconstruct the history of the school from its records as we organized the materials donated to the library. Here were two contemporaneous records of education of music students in Oregon, serious attempts within a rather small city to provide a creditable music education.

Music teachers (the older the better) became one of our best sources of information and materials. Almost all had gathered published teaching compositions, as well as more advanced sheet music for the piano, voice, violin, and other instruments. Some music was still valid for instructional use, while other pieces represented works and methods of another era. One teacher had become the national leader of a piano teaching method, having succeeded its deceased founder, and a record of her travels, texts on the Dunning system, sample keyboard exercises, and memorabilia are part of our library. While the teaching method originated in New York, it became a national success because of the leadership of our Portland subject.

Another music teacher led us to the music critics; in fact, her dearest friend was reviewer for a Portland newspaper. She had inherited his files when he died, and we were delighted to find a complete file of his reviews, as well as letters of inquiry, praise, and condemnation provoked by his statements. Our subject's collection leads to an understanding of the man—his favorite composers and performers, his preferred compositions, and his pet operas.

Another teacher had achieved a national reputation with the works she composed for piano. Many were published by Fischer and Schirmer, and many had provoked letters from performers and listeners. We have her working manuscripts, correspondence, publicity, and scrapbooks. The reputation of her music has lasted, even though her death occurred a good many years ago. To study her work is to learn much about her method, technique, and inspiration; to listen to her compositions is a joy.

Not all Oregon composers wrote serious music. One fellow from the cattle country on the far side of the mountains wrote country music in the 1910s, occasionally writing words to accompany the piano and/or guitar. He billed himself as the "poet lariat."

Another aspiring composer learned the hard way about music publishing. Her files of correspondence reveal the success of the vanity publisher whose advertisement offered a wide spectrum of possibilities. From the initial response to her inquiry through the many promotional prospects to the publisher's receipt of the check, we can read what has occurred. There are promises—to write words to accompany the music, to compose a song to accompany the lyrics, to publish the work as a piece of sheet music, to distribute the music to stores across the country, to cut and publicize a recording sent free to selected radio stations, and to promote the piece through performance by a top recording star. The half dozen cartons of correspondence show that our composer finally learned that her work was hopeless, but the value of the collection rests very much upon a history of the unscrupulous side of music publishing.

The lyricist, like Stoddard King, a reviewer and columnist for a Northwest newspaper, does meet with success on occasion. King will be remembered for "There's a Long, Long Trail A-Winding" long after his contributions to the newspaper have lost meaning except to the researcher. It was important to us, however, to try to secure as much material as possible, to see what made King a lyricist, poet, and composer; the bonus received with the gift was the long series of letters written by Vachel Lindsay to King.

The poet is often lyricist, and from Oregon's poet laureate, we learned a great deal about lyricists, or would-be lyricists, in the Northwest. The common attitude that "whatever I do is hard and whatever the other person does is easy" applies to the lyricist: he has written a poem, and almost anyone can then set it to music. It seemed that this was a common question posed to our poet laureate, and most dramatically at the time of a natural disaster or crisis. When President Kennedy was shot, people telephoned our poet to sing with or without background accompaniment what they had written as memorial tributes.

The individual, family, or group, whether formally trained or not, may demonstrate remarkable musical abilities. The DeMoss family, from the tiny town of DeMoss, Oregon, a good many miles from Portland, had been nationally famous as a touring company, the DeMoss Concert Entertainers, 1872-1932. They had kept journals, engagement books, contracts, correspondence, manuscript music, published works, testimonials, programs, handbills, photos, clippings, recordings, and mementos of travel. The collection was perfect for one of our students, Gay Grace Blankenship, whose master's thesis, *The DeMoss Family Musicians: Lyric Bards of Oregon*, shows Mrs. Blankenship's writing ability and the depth of the DeMoss papers.

Another family came to capitalize on its forebears; three generations had led orchestras, and three generations of scores and arrangements were stored in the attic when I first met the owner, a widow. She had no use for the collection, but we did. Here was music from the 1880s through the 1930s that had been played by three orchestras, the earliest based in Chicago, the second in Arizona, and the third in Portland. As time passed, the third group realized that what it possessed was popular for nostalgia purposes, and so, by the 1930s, it played "old time" music. The conductor's score and the musicians' arrangements make the collection a gem today.

Music from another era was that of a mandolin orchestra, popular at the turn of the century. The collection contained basically only arrangements, which delighted one of our faculty who had had his musical beginnings in just such a group. We courted for several years an elderly vaudeville performer whose scrapbooks contained programs, letters, small posters, original skits and compositions, and manuscript recollections of his life. A visit with the gentleman always entailed a bit of his dancing, a few snappy off-color jokes, and the promise that he would give those books to us on the next visit. He died without making the gift, and his nephew, who inherited the estate, destroyed the scrapbooks.

While we courted the vaudeville singer and dancer, we also met two other musicians whose work delighted the theater audience. One pianist had had her start with the silent movies, playing from scores provided for the films, but, more often, improvising and then transcribing her own scoring; we saved the worn fragments for the library. Another theater performer, the theater organist, had literally risen out of the pit to delight his audience; not only had he played for the audience, but, with an already assembled group, he performed his own compositions, which were to be published by recognized publishing houses. He had saved his published music and a few manuscripts, but totally lacking were the fan letters and publishers' correspondence that his work provoked.

In the 1930s, the federal Works Progress Administration supported formation of state or community bands and orchestras. The problem for our library was to discover what had become of its work; one library held transcriptions (16" slow-speed recordings), while another held some of the arrangements; programs and broadsides had been scattered to the winds, along with much material concerning the original pieces that had been commissioned. To reassemble its records is a continuing project.

While manuscript materials were our principal quest, we certainly were interested in other materials for the music collection. We secured from a major library its 78rpm classical record collection, and almost everyone seemed anxious to donate their 78rpm popular recordings to the library. One bachelor in Portland had spent his entertainment money exclusively on 78rpm albums, and his three-story home was full; there was little room for a table, chair, and bed. A major shopping center was about to purchase his property when we had the back-breaking job of removing his collection. A city physician had collected specific classical pieces as performed by as many orchestras and soloists as he could find. Recently one of our faculty asked for any recorded performance by a particular performer from the 1930s; a candidate for our school of music played in the style of the musician, and we had several concertos to lend.

Music stores not only have their own business accounts, but in several cases, they have provided treasures within our state. When killing time between meetings in a small town, I discovered in a junk store about 5,000 mint-condition 78rpm recordings from the late 1930s and early 1940s. I returned the next day with a station wagon to begin to haul the collection to the library; the secondhand store's owner was pleased to be relieved of his burden (the result of a bankrupt record store). A collection now in private ownership in the state was gathered by the owner of a cylinder record shop, who set aside for his personal pleasure one copy of each of about 6,000 items.

Concluding our personal views, not all situations turn out favorably. We were called in by a library that had been given a symphony's old scores and arrangements. The collection was vast and appeared extremely useful; however, the condition of the music was wretched, and parts were missing from every composition. It is important to assess the collection before accepting it.

CONTACTING THE POTENTIAL DONOR

Even though the program is conducted on a community basis and personal telephone solicitation seems easy, it is wise to introduce the library's music interests through correspondence. The potential donor may introduce himself, or be introduced, to the library, but it is still best to establish a working relationship through a letter that outlines the interests and intent of the library. Thus the donor receives a letter concerning content and use of the collection, as well as what the library hopes of him personally. A formal, printed invitation to donate may save the library time and effort; a telephone campaign may enlist the library's friends and volunteer help; but we feel strongly that nothing can substitute for a personal letter—a personal, direct invitation to the potential donor. The appendix contains several sample letters. They are intended as suggestions and should not be used verbatim.

POTENTIAL DONOR'S RESPONSE:
IS IT TIME TO MEET HIM?

If the donor responds by mail, the librarian has time to consider the response; if the donor telephones, it is easiest for the librarian to press for a meeting. The telephone conversation, if carried on at any length, provides too easy a means for the potential donor to dismiss the library request. He feels that he has had the courtesy to reply, even though in effect he has said "no." If the librarian has any suspicion that the donor has material, the librarian seeks a meeting, regardless of the information given over the telephone.

The donor's letter, on the other hand, is a more deliberate communication and probably indicates what the donor or musician's reaction has been: he has music but no correspondence; he is embarrassed by the messy way he has kept his work, but is willing to be visited; he will donate an old baton, if his children do not wish it; his work is set aside for another library; he has had too many bad experiences with municipal government; or he has destroyed everything. Each letter, regardless of its content, ought to be answered, with plans to meet its writer established or dismissed.

MEETING THE POTENTIAL DONOR

By arranging a meeting, the librarian becomes local emissary not only in terms of its music program, but as an informed representative of the community. Does he know what the city council has planned for the municipal auditorium? Is he aware of the school system's music program? Did he attend last evening's recital? As a public employee, his role seems much broader than that of the music collection's representative, ready to enrich the collection.

The librarian meets each potential donor with an open mind. If the donor's home, pets, politics, and musical tastes are not his own, he is careful not to indicate his concern or opinions. While visiting one piano teacher who helped us gain several major collections, I observed a statue atop the mantle. That statue eventually flew from its perch, and we admired the teacher's live pigeon. After learning of the skunk which lived beneath the sofa on which we had chosen to sit, we waited a decent interval before selecting another seat. Another donor interrupted his political harangue on the phone in order to answer our knock and then returned to the telephone. We very carefully avoided all talk of politics and focused our attention upon a good collection of sheet music.

The donor's collection may be stored in the piano bench, and the librarian waits until the donor moves off that bench before satisfying his curiosity; it may be on the top shelf of an unlit closet, and the librarian seeks the nearest chair and available light to assess the gift. He balances precariously to reach the furthest corners while worrying about dropping the heavy box of fragile cylinder records. Regard for his clothes is secondary to his mission in the attic or basement. He may compete actively, too, with the resident rodent population. The near-sighted violinist with severe halitosis and need for a complete change of clothing does not deter the librarian when he and the potential donor share the same small space to review in the strong box the choicest letters written to the once-famous musician.

A number of questions arise in the librarian's mind at the time of the interview: Is the potential donation within the scope of the collection? Are the donor's restrictions such that the librarian must reconsider? Is the gift available now, and can the librarian find the means to pack and move it immediately? Or, will the librarian need to court the potential donor, perhaps with a series of letters that rephrase the library's interest and its request, with references from other satisfied musicians, or with a letter or two from the chief librarian? Has he pressed too hard in his desire for the material?

After a personal appraisal of the potential donor and a professional evaluation of the music in question, the librarian considers other needs of the general library. He may observe a good book collection on musical history or theory, or one that is on a totally unrelated field but is of special interest to the library. The librarian must speak for this material, supporting his plea with mention of the library's interest in this area, perhaps due to budgetary problems, heavy use, or predicted demands. The librarian knows the scope of the music collection, and the depths, strengths, and weaknesses of the library itself.

The librarian must recognize when to be quiet and to listen to the musician, and when to draw out those details which may indicate the potential donor's plans or enable the librarian to learn both personally and professionally about another aspect of the community's musical heritage. He knows when to state his case, when to summarize the meeting, and when to leave, with or without his gift. Unless he wishes to promote the relationship, he terminates the solicitation meeting on a friendly but final basis. Should the performer have further gifts or have a supply of worthwhile leads, the librarian indicates that he will return.

The musician's questions may concern use, preservation, disposal, financial appraisal, or organization, while the librarian's responses reaffirm the original correspondence or open a new tack responding to some special question. In all cases, a follow-up letter repeats, clarifies, or develops the verbal discussion. The librarian will wish a formal record of his negotiations with the performer, musician, or his heirs.

PROCESSING THE COLLECTION: PUBLISHED MUSIC

On receipt of the gift in the library, the librarian has the opportunity to assess the gift, without need to flatter or please the donor and without the distraction that the surroundings and packing entail at the donor's home. In the case of sheet music, does he wish to arrange it by subject, instrument, date, composer, title, or some other means? Should each piece be fully cataloged, or should the collection be kept as a unit with an index? Should a record be kept if portions are removed for use elsewhere?

The librarian anticipates both present and future use, arranging the collection for easiest possible access. Often content dictates arrangement. Are the pieces regional, published locally? Are they commemorative, written about the same event, such as World War I? Are they all rags, marches, or ballads, written for the piano, piano and voice, or piano and violin, or other combinations? Can the gift be divided into obvious segments?

PROCESSING THE COLLECTION:
MANUSCRIPTS

If the collection is from a working composer or lyricist, it might be arranged in a manner similar to that discussed in the chapter concerning children's authors and illustrators. If the subject kept diaries or journals, they should be treated first. If the correspondence files are extensive, they should appear next. The creative individual's own work should then be included, based on either a chronological, alphabetical, or musical form arrangement. The choice of arrangement may depend on whether the music is undated and there is no way to establish dates. If the gift lacks much correspondence, perhaps letters should be included with the individual pieces, supporting the creation, performance, or publication of special compositions. Several sample inventories are included in the appendix.

The performer's files, whether he be vocalist, instrumentalist, or conductor, contain correspondence, fan letters, press clippings, tapes, or recordings, and sometimes printed or published music. The collection ought to be arranged according to the content and research value, from most to least important. If all parts were equally documented, the order would probably be: diaries or journals; correspondence; performed works including the music from which he performed and the tapes or recordings as well; less important would be the fan letters, press scrapbook, publicity photographs, and awards. The research value differs frequently from the performer's estimate of his materials; rave reviews, publicity photographs, and autographs from the celebrated are most important to the performer but seldom provide significant data for the researcher.

The critic or reviewer places most emphasis on published reviews, but the researcher hopes to find the critic's correspondence with others who discuss music, trends, personalities, and, in short, all the gossip that documents the social and professional aspects of the critic's life. A newspaper or journal file provides copies of the reviews, so again, in organizing the critic's collection, the librarian begins with correspondence.

The researcher's interest in files of a musical society or small music group will center about correspondence and/or works performed. The librarian generally organizes first the society's records or minutes of meetings and correspondence, and then the works performed. Publicity photographs, reviews, and fan letters interest him least, although these may be most interesting for display or illustration.

MAINTAINING DONOR INTEREST

A music collection gains importance and support as it contributes to public performance, study, and research. Through news notes, press releases, an occasional celebration, and perhaps library performance, public awareness of the collection increases. The donor's main satisfaction is often to see research based on his donation; occasionally his demand for appreciation is not satisfied unless his name is touted as donor, collector, and/or innovator.

Music in all forms lends itself to display. Many anniversaries, whether associated with music or not, have been commemorated by song. A disaster, political campaign, promotion, or social issue is almost always documented by an attractive piece of sheet music. An exhibition of music is easy to arrange, and the librarian's text can be minimal. The creative individual, composer, lyricist, or performer often leaves a colorful record, in terms of both letters and posters; a display of publicity photographs, programs, autographed letters, and several recordings is effective.

To encourage donor interest, the librarian keeps the donor informed of uses to which his gift is being put and of the plans that are projected. The donor may wish to assist the researcher with information or occasionally with finances. The librarian is the best judge of how frequently to keep his donor posted with current news.

Music is a fascinating subject area to collect. The librarian need not be a musician, but he must know the musician's language, music's role in community history, and what makes good research materials. The collection can be developed enthusiastically to encompass many aspects of community musical life, or, with the gift of files from a major orchestra, the library may have to restrict itself to that one collection due to space, funds, staff, and service. The decision is up to the individual library.

Chapter 11

THE BOOK GIFT

The story of a personal library is not unlike that of a private manuscript collection. Each is gathered over a limited period of years for a personal purpose; each is important to the collector (who may become donor or whose heirs may make the donation) during his most productive or creative period. With the waning of the donor's interest, as well as the loss of general concern for the subject, the books and manuscripts become less important and have less value. Often, shortly after the collector's death, both unpublished and published materials reach a low point in research value as well as monetary value. Generally the librarian enters at this moment and makes a critical decision: is the collection to be discarded and/or dispersed, or preserved? In this decision, however, he must weigh the phenomenon of cyclical value. In many disciplines, succeeding generations find new significance in what was written and discussed twenty-five or fifty years earlier. Manuscript and book collections often have a life cycle similar to man's, with the birth of an idea, its growth and conversion to manuscript form, eventual publication and promulgation, public recognition, use as a building block for further ideas, casual acceptance of the original contribution, waning interest, eventual demise of its authors, and the remaindering or destruction of the author's or collector's original creative efforts.

Occasionally, the soliciting librarian encounters a gift of books that are of more use and value than the manuscripts. He must be prepared for such a fortuitous situation. In view of the inflation of new and used book prices and curtailed library budgets, book gifts are especially desirable. The book allotment is the easiest budget item to cut without personnel adjustments or changes in service. Even when the initial effort to seek manuscripts from the potential donor leads to naught, it is wise to ascertain what books the potential donor has and to seek them actively, if they would be beneficial.

RELATING THE POTENTIAL GIFT
TO THE LIBRARY'S NEEDS

With specific knowledge of his collection, the librarian assesses the donor's books. The questions he responds to may be similar to the ones that follow, but, in each case, his questions and answers are suited to his individual library; there are few common or direct responses. Are there new or current titles that the library has yet to purchase, needed duplicate copies of recent best sellers, or standard sources that the library has been unable to purchase? Are there replacements for lost or mutilated items in art, photography, theater, ballet, sex, or local history; books to reinforce a subject area now ignored with the demise or departure of its proponent and purchaser, whether librarian, patron, or donor? Are there titles to fill the gap created during a period of curtailed budget when all books on certain subjects were automatically ignored? Does the donor's potential gift represent an area that the library has totally ignored and that has become a lively subject? Is there a run of a magazine to replace missing library copies, to complete the file begun only when the publication became "important," or to supply still another title indexed in the *Reader's Guide*? Could this collection furnish the bookmobile anticipated in the next fiscal year?

In addition to immediate uses, the librarian must consider fringe benefits. Will a portion be useful for exchange with other institutions or dealers, or a library book sale? Would the gift supply additional reading in a hospital, jail, retirement home, junior college, public school system, or similar institutions? Would this be a vital gift for a beginning library within the state or for a devastated library that has appealed widely to replace its lost collection? Would the books interest one of several agencies that distribute to foreign libraries?

PHYSICAL CONDITION OF THE BOOKS

The librarian who decides he wants the gift must pose another series of questions to himself, and these responses are often consistent from library to library. He wants to know whether the books will survive library use. Are they in need of repairs? Have they been overly read, or loved to death by children? Did the donor or his friends underline or highlight the text, write marginal comments, fold down the corners, use paper clips (now well rusted)? Did the donor's children do their own illustrating with crayon or ink? Are there signs of mutilation—plates, illustrations, or maps removed or poems clipped out? Often the answer to mutilation is displayed on the donor's walls, and asking the donor about the plates may save the librarian much collation. Will the books be worth processing in spite of the condition? At what point is it better to purchase a new copy than to process an unattractive copy with a short shelf life?

In addition to damage from personal use, problems may arise from improper storage: dry rot, moisture, heat, cold, and uneven temperatures cause paper and bindings to deteriorate. The books may have been subjected to city grime, water, or fire damage. Silverfish, mice, rats, or even moths may have taken personal possession of the collection. The donor may have provided special care for his books by putting them into plastic bags, ignoring the moisture level in the air and in the books when he stored them, and the result may be mildew or rot. He may have placed his library in cartons, and, if they were stored properly with protective paper, the books will survive well. If, however, a tenant dumped the books into cartons during the collector's absence, the resultant warped bindings and broken spines are evident.

The donor may have practiced elementary binding, perhaps destroying good books through insufficient binding skills or placing an attractive binding on a cheap reprint with paper of poor quality. The binder tries his binding skills but does not exercise the art of selection. His books must be collated—title pages and plates checked and even reviewed to see that the contents are the same as the spine label. The propensity to bind may lead to made-up volumes composed of fragments of once sound monographs.

TERMS OF THE GIFT

If the library does want the books, the librarian must learn whether the donor wishes to place special restrictions on his gift. If the librarian were to pose the following questions to the donor, the library staff would be swamped with work, much of it excessive in relation to the value of the gift.

The librarian should be alert to the possibilities as he listens to the donor. Does the donor want a bookplate to be put in each volume, and will that plate have a sensible inscription—one that will look appropriate 25 or 50 years from the date of the gift? Does he wish to establish a memorial shelf with a static collection containing only the present donation? This gift will appear dated and useless 25 or 50 years from now, and in the meantime, he is seriously limiting accessibility and therefore use. Is he willing to allow the library to dispose of unwanted or duplicate items through gift, exchange, sale, or pulping (destruction)? Is he concerned with promoting a special interest—religious doctrine, political theory, or local issues? Does he desire a detailed listing of all books, an appraisal paid for by the library, and public recognition? Does the library have staff, time, and space to select, evaluate, process, and house the gift? The librarian volunteers those suggestions which he feels appropriate for the specific gift.

DONORS

The book collector, researcher, or writer who has assembled a library is a wonderful donor. He knows what he has, its intrinsic and monetary value, its gaps, quality, and depth, names of specialized dealers, authorities in the field, and friends with similar collecting tastes. He knows publishers, editions, and reprints. From such collectors, the librarian enriches his knowledge of the field. The librarian can speak more directly to the collector, seeking information and, occasionally, financial support. The collector knows what the librarian wants and why; his has been a similar motivation, as we have said in an earlier chapter.

The donor who is unfamiliar with an inherited collection is a study in contrasts. Too often his curiosity is kindled initially when the librarian expresses interest. Previously, the books represented a burden—they collected dust and grime and were a space problem—but now they have become important. The donor may express himself in several ways, each to become familiar to the solicitor. "My uncle loved fine literature and read every volume. How much is this worth? Is that a first edition? I want to give that to a friend. Is this textbook (1910 vintage) a rare book? How amazing! I never knew my uncle had so many interests, and, in fact, I know him better now by looking at his books than when I used to visit him." The librarian is privy to the donor's excitement and is distracted in his attempt to evaluate the shelves for his own needs. He should gain time to examine the collection, perhaps by asking the donor to look at several books of special interest but of inconsequential importance to the library.

The family library often reflects the interests of the family members and a myriad of casual interests—books promoted on television or otherwise widely popularized; texts needed to solve a home plumbing or carpentry problem; escape reading for vacation or a long plane trip; volumes delivered regularly from a book club; craft or hobby books; light fiction plus a few titles for spiritual, emotional, or educational enrichment; and children's books worn to shreds, colored by several generations, mended with adhesive tape first, and re-mended with Scotch tape. Later we will discuss one such book, a textbook, and why it has survived within a family library.

BOOK SELECTION, EVALUATION, AND ASSESSMENT

Viewing the potential gift brings specific questions to the librarian's mind in addition to those discussed in "Relating the Potential Gift to the Librarian's Needs." Each question pertains to the library's special goals. What is the subject of the gift? How do the books relate to the manuscript collection, the original reason for the librarian's meeting? Is the librarian able to assume that the books are considered as part of his original request? Are the books in-depth studies or merely superficial overviews? Are they cheap reprints or original editions? Were they bought for an immediate professional need, or were they gathered over a long period of time? Were they purchased as an investment or for fine bindings, steel engravings, or subject matter? Do they represent a twenty-year membership in the Literary Guild or Book-of-the-Month Club, or a series of bargains from remainder lists? If they are completely unfamiliar, are they of special interest to the library? The librarian checks authors, titles, publishers, dates, indices, bibliographies, and contents.

Have the books retained a sound value in spite of their age, or do they reflect only the taste and popularity of the period when they were assembled? Are they so dated that they assume a new value as an historical record of another era? We once encountered a collection built between 1860 and 1880, with no volumes of current interest; the books, however, were an accurate picture of contemporary reading tastes, combined with a segment of unread, self-uplifting volumes. Does an historical anniversary herald a renewed interest or evoke nostalgia in a subject or author? Having collected for over twenty years, we have witnessed a resurgence of readers devoted to the Spanish-American War, Civil War, Rudyard Kipling, astrology, composting, Lafcadio Hearn, vegetable gardens, World War II, and so on. What may be a static collection at the moment may become the library's desiderata within five years. Can the librarian anticipate future demands?

The librarian reviews authors represented in the potential gift. Are they contemporary specialists within their fields, or popularizers? Are they respected still, or passé? Have they been collected in depth? If the librarian recognizes only half the titles by one author, the chances are good that he will secure the lesser works of the author, as well as duplicates of those familiar to him. Does he ignore good reading copies of Melville, Steinbeck, or Dreiser, or replace the library's worn copies? Often the librarian has only one opportunity to select—he must rapidly evaluate the collection before him, inform the donor of his decision, and not await reinforcement from the social science expert, the reader's adviser, or the music librarian. He may well lose the potential gift by delay.

Most books are first editions, never having been through a second printing and yet the donor may wax enthusiastic about his "firsts" which in reality lack literary, historical, and/or financial value. If the librarian hears little but extravagant praise, he may wish to refuse the gift, realizing the shock and disbelief a frank statement would create in the donor's mind. The librarian has the experience, plus his bibliographic sources, to authenticate and evaluate first editions, but the donor learns about first editions through a popular news story or the ignorance of an unbookish friend. Many times we have seen a "first edition" of *Robinson Crusoe*, *Les Misérables*, Dante's *Inferno*, or *Faust*, published in New York by A. L. Burt or P. F. Collier, firms recognized for their cheap printings for mass markets. Common sense often dictates what may be important firsts: do date, language, place, and publisher seem right?

Old books may have financial value in the donor's eyes—the older the volume and the younger the donor, the greater he will imagine the cash value. The concept has little validity. Too frequently the volumes are old textbooks or pirated editions, such as those mentioned above, "borrowed" by American publishers of the last century for mass sales without concern for the author's rights or even the authenticity of the text. Such books are sometimes recognized by cheap bindings and poor paper, and yet they were retained as family treasures. Indeed, their importance is purely for family association value. The librarian prefers to watch for works from the nineteenth century publishers like Tichnor and Fields, Harper, Lothrop and Lee, issued with good bindings and paper.

JUDGING A BOOK BY ITS COVER

In reviewing a gift, the librarian can judge certain things almost immediately by bindings, despite the old adage. Spine design, binding, and typog-
raphy among certain publishers have varied little over the years. The Victorian
binding stands out, regardless of the content; the unimaginative, cheap spine
of the turn-of-the-century novel indicates the subject; Prentice-Hall, Irwin,
Ginn, McGraw-Hill, and Heath suggest to the eye today the dull content of
the textbook of yesterday. Giving only a hasty glance to the bindings, the
librarian gains a sense of the quality and subject matter before him. If that
judgment is too negative, he will proceed with more care, hoping to find
that the old adage was indeed correct. He learns within his own library to
recognize publishers, subjects, and period by spine.

Donations may include handsomely bound sets of standard or little
read authors. The donor values highly his sets to the exclusion of pamphlets,
journals, and even monographs; that estimation may be placed on the wrong
materials. *Messages and Papers of the Presidents*, Stoddard's *Lectures*, leather-
bound nineteenth century encyclopedias, miscellaneous federal document
sets, and "limited editions" of great British, French, and German novelists
and historians appear imposing on the donor's shelves. The eight-, twelve-,
or twenty-volume set is too often little more than a piece of furniture. The
set may carry an indication of "limited edition," number such-and-such of a
total of 500 copies. This attracted the buyer years ago and still deceives today's
buyer. That particular set may have been issued in various formats and forms
with differing title pages, paper, bindings, and edition statements. The spine
is alluring, but the content is uninspiring.

During the eighteenth century, a good many cheap leather-bound editions of standard works appeared in Europe. In the following century, leather
was used to bind religious and moral treatises, works of respectable British
poets and novelists, and the common reference work. While the leather spine
deserves attention, the librarian should restrain his enthusiasm until he
examines the contents.

Subscription books, books sold door-to-door in the late nineteenth and
early twentieth centuries, were designed to appeal to the purchaser who
sought a compendium of knowledge, a code of manners and etiquette, and
the memorial volume commemorating a national disaster or the death of a
notable leader. The appealing cover, often with an illustration, the larger-
than-average format, and the choice of binding provided the purchaser with

a respectable library. Such acquisitions included a book on McKinley's assassination, the Galveston disaster, war in the Philippines, the Johnstown Flood, the principles of elocution, and a handbook of social manners. Because these were often the only books purchased, and, because of their enduring, imposing appearance, subscription books have survived in great numbers. Unless the librarian is gathering volumes to reflect a turn-of-the-century household library, his problem today is one of tact: how does he refuse the gift, and, further, if called upon for some financial estimate, what is he to say?

Similarly, the door-to-door salesman sold "mug books," which we have discussed as a source of leads. Mug books, because of a restricted sale within a community or county or state, are scarce and expensive today. The library can almost always use another copy to replace a worn or mutilated copy. It is still possible to predict in older, stable regions of the country which middle-class families purchased and preserved the efforts of the commercial travelers.

AN ECONOMICS TEXTBOOK, PUBLISHED IN 1927: AN EXAMPLE

Let us consider an economics textbook, written in 1927 (one of many that year written for college freshmen). The book contained the best information available then, but it is badly dated now. Is its author still important? Does the book have a valid bibliography? Is the text a classic? Will the volume become important again historically? The answers are probably negative. The book represents economics as it was taught on a beginning level in 1927. We selected 1927 because that date approximates the date of textbooks currently received as gifts.

The date reflects the age of the donor who was in college or high school in 1927. His family is grown, retirement is imminent, and a move to smaller quarters is often predictable. He may have realized that he never will reread the text nor use it for reference, and he may further recognize that the subject has changed since 1927. On the other hand, he may have a different attitude. He recalls purchasing the book, a substantial purchase for a young man. He did not wish to buy the $1.50 text but was compelled to do so. With inflation and the age of the book, it has become in the donor's mind much more significant in both price and content. He feels that the text is a classic, influencing not only his generation, but his children's. The librarian may have to discuss the matter with tact, for that costly book has become precious to the donor.

In either case, whether the donor has come to recognize both his limitations and those of the book, or whether he feels he possesses The Book, the owner escapes the sacrilege of discarding the book by offering it to the library.

The library rarely wants such a text. Should the librarian explain why his library does not wish the book? If he must, the librarian speaks as a professional on behalf of his institution, not as an antiquarian dealer who knows financial values. The librarian may suggest that the donor give the text to his grandchildren as something representative of his college years; it may have a sentimental value to an older grandchild. He may also suggest that his alma mater might collect textbooks used in its earlier years. It is possible, too, with tact, to say directly that economics has changed in concept and philosophy over the last fifty years, and thus the book represents but one student text among the thousands since published.

It may be that the donor wishes the librarian to admire his gem while he is anxious to have everything else hauled off. The librarian in relief may be willing to respond to the donor's question about a local bindery to repair this battered text. Occasionally, the donor may pit the librarian against his alma mater, where he knows "his" library is anxious for his volume. Each situation demands an individual course of action. What are the donor's intentions? Is it best to accept the economics text in order to secure dozens of worthwhile books, with never an indication that the donor has chosen the worst possible book on which to focus the bookish discussion? Is the economics text but one representative of an overvalued, outdated collection?

ACCEPTANCE OR REFUSAL

Although the librarian may simply have been asked to admire the books while securing the manuscript gift, he must assess the gift possibilities and take an aggressive posture if the collection is of merit. Equally, he ought to be prepared to offer advice if it is sought, when the collection is of no interest to the library.

If the books are not available but good, does the donor wish to sell them? The librarian might suggest several members of the Antiquarian Booksellers Association of America (ABAA) whose shops are nearby or whose specialties encompass the donor's collection. Suggesting more than one name is important, so that the librarian is not charged with collusion.

If the volumes are not worth much in financial terms, or if a dealer is remote from the collection, the librarian might suggest private sale, perhaps through an advertisement in the newspaper or on the radio. The librarian may personally think that the books are definitely inferior and that any dealer would be dismayed were he to journey to examine the books; again, the librarian would emphasize local private sale. Such a negotiation would benefit both buyer and seller, if each concedes his amateur status. The seller gains an advantage by securing more than he would receive from a dealer, while the buyer purchases at a price lower than what he would pay for the same volumes from the shelves of a used bookstore. Such sales often include book club novels or non-fiction, large sets of American or British authors, *American Heritage, National Geographic, Horizon,* or the eclectic assemblage of a reading family. In such negotiations, the librarian refrains from the role of financial expert. His library has reference sources for the buyer and seller to use.

GIFT BOOK POLICY

The librarian should use his tact, ability, diplomacy, and wit to suggest appropriate disposition of material which neither he nor the donor wishes. To burden another library, institution, or dealer in order to avoid disparaging the donor's books is neither proper nor professional. To suggest several solutions, when asked, produces a rapport between the donor and the library. We have mentioned various means of disposal in this chapter: retention within the family for personal or sentimental purposes, sale to a dealer or private party, donation to another institution, or, when fitting, actual discard.

To rely on a written gift book policy statement to discourage unwanted or undesirable donations provides escape and protection for the librarian. However, the donor receives the impression that he has dealt with another governmental agency where red tape prevails, an agency which had sought his material, only to insult him with its refusal carefully spelled out in a policy statement.

CONCLUSION

It is our personal lament that too few book buyers are interested in selecting their own book purchases. On one hand, the book club provides a steady flow of current, popular, fashionable reading in diverse fields; on the other, the use of current common review media and weekly book ratings does much to popularize and distribute a very limited number of titles. Many good books published each year are lost in the morass of volumes not promoted by clubs, reviewers, advertising, television interviews, and rating charts. The discerning reader, who purchases books on the strength of his knowledge, taste, and depth of interest, creates a library of scholarly and financial value that brings joy to the heart of the librarian.

Chapter 12

PROFESSIONAL AND PERSONAL QUALITIES

The qualities and talents described below represent an ideal. The woman or man who seeks a position as manuscripts solicitor or field representative might consider some of the aspects described as potential goals.

THE SOLICITOR:
FORMAL AND PERSONAL REPRESENTATIVE OF THE LIBRARY

The librarian who initiates a program needs to believe firmly in the program, to know his fields well, to have the support of administration and associates, to possess confidence in himself, and to accept his responsibility and obligations to both the library and donors without measuring hours worked or work performed. The librarian becomes in the donor's eyes an extension of the institution and, thus, must be responsive to all his questions, complaints, thoughts, and problems. The relationship between the donor and the library is a personal one, with the librarian acting as intermediary. The donor has given something very special; his records or family files represent a precious part of his self-concept, and he needs reassurance that his gift will be treated well.

Resourceful talents are demanded for any number of special services: entertaining a visitor without quite knowing who the guest is or what he might possess of research value, securing whatever the donor seeks in terms of information from the library or its parent institution, listening appreciatively to the donor's concerns, but remaining quiet unless advice is specifically sought in an area of professional competence. Weekends, evenings, breakfast-time must be available if that is what the benefactor wishes. In many situations, the librarian supplants family or fulfills a missing family role, and he must be careful not to be monopolized by the lonesome contributor anxious for some social contact, family companionship, or a regular free meal.

The librarian must flexibly adapt his schedule to that of others to avoid conflict with a hairdresser appointment, a chess game, or lawn bowling match; such scheduling may seem trivial, but daily routine is important to the donor. The businessman may seem to be doing nothing behind his closed door, but the librarian might make three attempts to find him available.

Patience in this situation is important, as it is when the librarian becomes the willing listener. The prospective donor often feels that the librarian shares his political, religious, ethnic, or social persuasion. Sometimes, if the librarian's patience is worn thin, or if he sees a danger in being accepted as a confrère, he must express himself with diplomacy, respecting the donor's beliefs, but stating that as a librarian he appreciates many differing viewpoints as well. He has, after all, approached the potential donor because of his professional concern in seeing the donor's view represented in the library. If the librarian does not speak out eventually, and if the donor feels that the library endorses his personal beliefs, the donor may inform others that the institution supports his philosophy.

PROFESSIONAL ATTITUDE, INTELLECTUAL CURIOSITY, AND INTUITION

The librarian's personal enthusiasm and interest move the donor to explore the hidden recesses of his home or office, draw the donor out to supply further details or material, and provoke a good gift, rather than the token originally planned by the donor. The librarian's enthusiasm, fed by earlier success, supports him when one or two meetings do not consummate the gift. The same positive attitude helps him crawl through an unlit cellar or a mouse-infested, leaky eaves closet in search of the donor's treasure. The cleaning bill or the cost of new clothes should not deter the librarian from securing the gift. When exploring a new situation, the librarian rids himself of preconceived notions about the donor and his gift, since preconceptions result in surprises.

The librarian's responsibilities determine his actions. Does the potential donor expect too much in return for his donation to the library? Does the gift belong in the library, or would it be better elsewhere? Does the gift have a sizeable cash value and is the donor in poor financial circumstances: should the librarians suggest purchase by the library or sale through a reputable dealer? Does the library have the facilities to take care of this much bulk, or the users to justify the donation? Is the gift simply a fragment or token wished upon the library by the donor? Can the gift be processed well and promptly, not stored in a basement for forty or sixty years waiting staff time for assembling and inventorying? In essence, the librarian has given his word that the collection will be arranged, inventoried, cataloged, appraised, and properly used.

This personal responsibility begins when the library selects the intellectually curious librarian to collect within a given field. The librarian is a walking card catalog, as we have said. He attempts to correlate that knowledge with what he collects. Seeking out information from his donors, users, and associates, the sleuth, or librarian, is responsible for special familiarity with the subject area. He builds from experience and research, gaining further insight into the field. He delves into allied subjects with the hope of increasing his own knowledge and background.

The librarian reads constantly, casting an eye toward the potential gift and keeping abreast of library donors to inform them of happenings or congratulate them on new publications. By reading unusual collections of letters, diaries, unpublished autobiographies, recollections, or essays, the librarian learns more about the donor and potential donor and becomes aware of other materials or subjects that have been neglected. From each collection come new ideas, thoughts, and leads. The librarian is resourceful and interested in researching and enriching his professional goals, both on and off the job.

In field work, the intuitive librarian develops a feeling for the situation— what the meeting entails, how to work with the donor, how to secure the gift, when to ask for the gift, and/or how to refuse the material. He learns to distinguish between the useful, informative donor and the one whose suggestions are poor, due to ignorance, misinformation, or a misconception of the library's collecting program. The librarian knows when to talk and when to listen.

ABILITY TO MAKE PROFESSIONAL DECISIONS

The librarian is understanding or aggressive, depending upon the situation. Knowing when to suggest that the impoverished donor sell rather than donate, or recognizing the emotional tie between the donor and material, along with the donor's definite intention of making the gift, takes special ability. The librarian may have to "sell" hard to secure a collection, if he sees that the donor lacks appreciation for the good material he possesses. The librarian tries to prevent the individual from destroying it, giving it to his grandchildren to take to school, or burdening a local library that has no way to care for it. The ideal solicitor needs to remember, too, to stop "selling" when he has misunderstood the potential donor's intent, when he meets a donor who is disinterested, turned off by the solicitor, antagonistic toward the institution, or in a negative frame of mind for reasons never to be learned.

The librarian who worries about the dignity and respect due his professional status should choose another area of work. He cannot be too important to get dirty, face a boring donor, meet an unfortunate situation, or pack and transport large, heavy shipments. The specialist anxious to build his library will commit himself readily to such a price. He should willingly work almost anywhere with anyone, when the collection is sufficiently promising. He may disdain, dislike, or hate the situation or the potential donor, but he should swallow his pride or snobbery, if he is committed to the program.

His professional pride should not preclude the realization that the donor can educate the librarian; the creative person knows his field, recognizes the materials most useful to him, and can explain why he has established this particular order of priorities. The librarian may then realize that these same priorities would be very important to the future user, and that the library should accept a type of material that it had previously ignored.

Professional memberships in scholarly associations, in bibliographical societies, and in similar organizations as well as civic groups bring the librarian in contact with many whose interests are similar to his or who find his work intriguing. The exchange of information, development of leads and associations, and enhancement of the library's status are benefits. The librarian is cautioned, however, to evaluate the friendship and concern of those anxious to assist him; he may be overwhelmed with potential donors of inconsequential materials, leads to and suggestions about matters of insignificant consequence, or visitors whose understanding and appreciation of the library are and remain nil. While many leads can occur from professional or personal associations, even from individuals whose possibilities seem very limited, the librarian must assess the source of information and make a decision as to whether he has time to cultivate the individual.

While lasting benefits do occur from the long-term cultivation of a donor, reaching beyond the walls of the library proper, the librarian's immediate responsibilities are to his library. If the art museum rejects a painting from the donor, the anthropology department spurns an artifact, and the English department informs the library's donor of its scorn for American detective fiction, the solicitor is forced to realize that he collects for the library alone. He should draw upon outside support only when he is certain of it, from administration and associates. On the other hand, a cash bequest to the art museum or anthropology or English departments will gain the library immediate support. The continued cultivation of a donor, drawing on appropriate support and interests when the librarian is assured of proper response, may well lead to long-term benefits to the institution, if not to the library.

The ability to make professional decisions on whether to cultivate the donor or simply to acknowledge receipt of the gift is one gained through experience. Over a period of years the librarian will think of the long-term gains for his institution, as well as of the immediate benefits to his library.

PERSONAL QUALITIES

Good grooming and respectful manners impress the donor. Wear neat and serviceable clothing for use in a basement, garage, or on a ladder. Avoid alcoholic beverages before visiting a good Methodist minister. Avoid profanity when dealing with a kindly, elderly soul. The donor is generally of a "respectable age" and would like to see the librarian "properly" dressed. The old-fashioned physician's bedside manner is something to be cultivated.

Personal financial obligations are rarely assumed by the publicly supported library. Attic work and dirty clothes mean cleaning bills. The replacement of clothes ripped by nails, spoiled by liquids, or torn by rough boards is a part of the job. The librarian pays for a token gift taken to the donor. While most potential donors assume that the librarian has a substantial travel account for entertainment, the dinner check is usually the personal responsibility of the librarian whose funding depends upon public support. The librarian buys the donor dinner or cocktails, although he does not indicate that his costs are not reimbursed by the library.

As a walking travel agent, the librarian knows the towns and cities he visits, at least by carrying maps and guides which enable him to find quickly the donor and a place from which to ship the donation. Prior to the trip, he locates all donors on the map and prepares an itinerary with appropriate information on appointments, locations, motels, and telephone numbers. He may carry the *Official Airline Guide* with him, in case he needs to change plane schedules. He has secured motel and car rental credit cards. He keeps abreast of car rental specials, motel chains with free reservation services, excursion plane fares, and any details that can minimize his travel costs.

PERSONAL INTEGRITY

The librarian, as representative of the library and of the institution, must have integrity. The gift being made is not a personal gift, although the donor may talk to the solicitor as if the gift belonged to him personally. The collector who acts as a solicitor for a library must have strict ethics and set aside his personal interests for those of his library. As a representative, he must use that ethical background, too, in responding and acting for his entire institution, not just the library. If he is not informed in the matter of municipal government, a development in the community college, or the economic situation within the county government, upon his return to the library, he had better prepare a good response, drawn from information sought from the authorities in the parent institution. As a representative of the library profession, he needs to be familiar with its recent developments, its history, and others who collect manuscripts.

The child who enters the candy shop is not unlike the librarian who discovers a multitude of riches when he meets his potential donor for the first time. Both are anxious to sample everything, but in reality, the librarian needs to know what has first priority for his library. After working with the donor, he returns to the library with the same delight and enthusiasm as the child: this collection will be his; he will put it into shape, based on the knowledge secured from working with the donor, and then write a book or article on the subject. Reality dictates the impracticality of the matter. He will not have time to carry through the project, and his responsibility may end with acquiring, organizing, or servicing the gift. It does not extend to using the collection for the purpose for which it was collected—to benefit present and future scholars.

On sabbatical leave, I met with librarians who had responsibilities similar to mine. Many manuscript solicitors were administrative officers whose prestigious title of head librarian encouraged gifts. In other libraries, the solicitor-librarian was tucked behind the scenes, his role so underplayed that gifts seemed to have been deposited on the library doorstep.

SUMMARY

The active librarian ought to find his position challenging, with the excitement of the chase, the surprise of a fine gift, and the demands of honor and integrity. He seeks a major gift intelligently, handles it properly, and sees that the donor is treated with the same respect and appreciation given his collection. The passive librarian can remain at his desk and receive whatever material is offered; such unsolicited gifts generally contain old text books, book club books, promotional pamphlets, and popular magazines. The intelligent, aggressive librarian opens new areas of study through manuscript work, securing new collections by means of his expertise and research. He meets many fine people and interesting specialists, anxious to share their knowledge with him, and, through the library, with others. His donors may well become his friends, and his life is enriched by these special friendships.

Chapter 13

BENEFITS GAINED FROM A SOLICITATION PROGRAM

DIRECT BENEFITS

A library that embarks on a serious collecting program benefits in several direct ways. The acquisition of fine gifts enhances the value of the library collection, attracts solicited and unsolicited gifts, and increases the library's stature and prestige in terms of its specialized collections. Its present users find far more primary and secondary materials, and new users are attracted to the library.

A good program develops a lively, interested group of donors who are anxious to assist "their" library and their gifts through additional contributions, suggestions of other possible donors, and, sometimes, financial and political support. The contributor's recommendation to professional associates and friends by word of mouth or letter is a form of public relations that money cannot secure. Both the library and its parent administrative body benefit directly and indirectly. The donor has given part of his life's work, and this contribution in kind—personal files, diaries, and letters—binds him tightly to the library. He has a personal stake in the library, and, more broadly, in the governing body.

We have met many alumni who have been annoyed by previous appeals for funds but who have greeted the library's request for materials as something special and deserving. The librarian's personal approach reflects a new institutional interest, directed at a practical concern—gifts of books and manuscripts. The alumnus is flattered and anxious to share his materials with the library. A similar attitude may exist toward county or municipal government, but a gift to the county or city library provides a new personal identification with the institution, as long as the library continues to maintain its good donor relations. A satisfied donor can be a welcome asset in a time of political or financial library crisis.

Research based on manuscript collections encourages users who had not been aware of the library's potentials. In turn, their studies are contributed to local, regional, or national publications, gaining further recognition for the library program, collections, and the parent institution. The librarian promotes the manuscript materials by making certain that information appears in the card catalog, by preparing finding aids and inventories, and by reporting acquisitions to *The National Union Catalog of Manuscript Collections.* The researcher appreciates the librarian who makes materials available as quickly as possible.

Books that cannot be purchased with a limited library budget may be acquired through solicitation. In our state university, we have no funds to buy books on pets, gardening, cooking, crafts, and other non-academic subjects. The smaller library can swell its reference shelves with a gift from someone who has had to purchase a good many basic reference tools for a project he has now completed. The metropolitan library can build its collection on immigrants when it secures the papers of a sociologist whose specialties included the immigrant in America.

FUTURE, INTANGIBLE BENEFITS

A bequest may provide future benefits—including the remainder of the collection, a sum of money, or the contents of a home, which might furnish a special meeting room, a leisure reading area, or a staff lounge.

The solicitation program, as we have said earlier, may rectify past wrongs, and, while the infraction may have been committed by either the library or the parent institution, it is often the library, working on a direct personal basis, that regains a favorable position. If the original problem were legitimate and could now be rectified, so much the better; if there were no solution, perhaps the passage of time and a new face representing the library could make some amends to provoke that gift or bequest once tentatively offered.

Philosophically, the benefits from a collecting program extend far beyond the library and the institution. The potential donor recognizes the possible value of his manuscripts due to the librarian's inquiry, and, as a result, he may then contact a neighboring library or his alma mater, with acceptance of the gift almost a foregone conclusion. While the innovative librarian has lost a collection, he has provoked the potential donor into action, and the material has been saved.

In the same manner, the letters or visits to a young, creative writer, musician, economist, or environmentalist may awaken an interest in saving files, in sparing them as he moves about. The younger person receives a tutorial session on preservation of working materials—why, how, what, and, the librarian hopes, where to place them eventually. A part of the librarian's role is that of missionary, and he can only hope that his labors will benefit some library in twenty or forty years.

Collecting broadly by subject or era or event creates a democratic collection, representing many points of view, from the most biased to the more philosophical attitude bent on accepting all viewpoints. We sometimes wonder about all those politicians, religious thinkers, doctrinaires, conservatives, and radicals so carefully housed on our shelves; it is a wonder that on long, dark nights sparks do not fly among them.

IMMEDIATE BENEFITS

From the narrowest standpoint, the library may well recoup its investment in staff, travel, and materials, if the librarian becomes a scrounger. The cabinets and store rooms of the library will overflow if the librarian secures all those supplies available when the donor is making his gift: paper clips, pencils, rubber bands, paper, pens, scratch pads, envelopes, three-ring binders, tape, clip binders, folders, card boxes, typewriters, typewriter ribbon, chairs, tables, glue, file cabinets, clocks, desks, book cases, transfer files, picture frames, rugs. The donor is ready to give; is the librarian ready to consider all of the library's needs?

SUMMARY

The librarian hopes to see his library become noted for its special manuscript collections, with supporting books, serials, and pamphlets. The institution should draw users, students, and scholars from the world of learning to benefit, in turn, through lectures, publications, or added research, the library, its parent institution, and society in general.

He hopes to see, as the result of his personal endeavors, the user brought together with the primary research materials which he secured and felt to be of sufficient value for permanent preservation. He hopes too that the future researcher may one day pause to consider why and how the gift was secured.

The small manuscript solicitation program provides an intellectual satisfaction based on the fruition of all its aspects, development of leads, solicitation of the donor, acquisition and organization of the gift, and eventual use by an intelligent researcher.

LIST OF APPENDICES

Appendix 5-1   Initial Letter
       (Material sought concerns local natural history)

   5-2   Initial Letter
       (Material sought is professional correspondence,
       files, working notes, and manuscripts)

   5-3   Initial Letter
       (Pitfalls)

   5-4   Second Letter
       (A reminder that the library has received no response)

Appendix 6   Field Notes

Note: Appendices' numbers (i.e., 5-1, 10-2) relate to chapters in the text. The second part of the number (i.e., -1, -2) refers to the order in which the reference appears within the chapter.

Appendix 7-1   Sample Receipt of Gift

          7-2   Sample Deed of Gift
                       (Musician and/or composer)

          7-3   Sample Deed of Gift

          7-4   Box Identification Label

          7-5   Progress of Manuscript Arrangement Form

          7-6   Collection Inventory Sample

          7-7   Collection Inventory Sample

          7-8   Collection Inventory Sample

          7-9   Biographical Information for Preparation of
                       Manuscript Inventories

Appendix 8-1   Name Card

          8-2   Geographical Card
                       (Lead card)

          8-3   Come-up, Tickler, or Reminder File, Based on a
                       Calendar Arrangement

Appendix 10-1   Policy

         10-2   Solicitation Letter to a Composer

         10-3   Solicitation Letter to a Musician

         10-4   Sample Pages of a Detailed Inventory

         10-5   Sample Cursory Inventory

Appendix 5-1

INITIAL LETTER
(Material sought concerns local natural history)

Dr. Thomas Jones
123 Rolling Hills Drive
Zenith, Wisconsin

Dear Dr. Jones:

For the last two years, as a response to community requests and needs,
our public city library has sought to build its collection of records relating to
the natural history of the area. Frank Smith suggested that we write to you
about our interest in your work as a student of local natural history.

We have received as gifts several collections of special importance to our
region: the books and pamphlets of Sallie Goforth, whose classes in field
botany were so long popular in town; the diaries and field notes of the late
ornithologist, Tom Burroughs; the photographic negatives and slides of botanist, Daisy Fleur; and the remarkable files and minutes of the Flora and Fauna
Club, whose secretary had saved them for many, many years.

These records have already served the community for serious studies, one to protect the Clear River, which is now a bill pending in Congress; another sponsored by the high school senior class to present an ecological picture of our town in 1900; and still another, by the Audubon Club, to document a remarked increase in the starling population.

Your files—that is, letters, notes, and field studies—would represent to both our present and future users a major contribution to the study of our region. We can assure you of the library's sincerity by preparing a full inventory of your gift for your own use and in order to provide users with knowledge of the contents of your gift.

It would be a pleasure to meet with you to discuss our suggestion.

Sincerely,

Appendix 5-2

INITIAL LETTER
(Material sought is professional correspondence, files, working
notes, and manuscripts)

Dr. Thomas Jones
123 Rolling Hills Drive
Zenith, Wisconsin

Dear Dr. Jones:

Zenith University has long sought records of the early leaders of the development of American sociology, and it is because of our recent acquisition of the John T. Smith papers that we write you. We find that the exchange of letters that you shared with Dr. Smith is one of the finest, most perceptive series to discuss contemporary sociology. Your ability to analyze the principal figures, trends, and publications, as well as to predict future trends, causes us to speak on behalf of our library.

Zenith's sociology collection, as you know, is remarkably good; not only do we have the basic source materials, such as texts, studies, and journals, but the manuscript collection has been built to reflect the leaders of the profession. Thus, we have acquired the papers of Alpha Beta Otto, Otto Alpha Beta, and Beta Otto Alpha, whose contributions to the field are well known. Each collection receives the usual library treatment: it is organized as a unit, inventoried, and used for serious research. Location of the collection is reported through the journal publications in your field, as well as to the Library of Congress.

We would ask you to consider placing your working records, such as letters, notes, lecture files, position papers, drafts, and working manuscripts in our library when any segment of the material is no longer useful to you. We realize that many scholars are plagued by too many old files, and we hope that we may serve as both your archives and your secretary in handling this older material.

We hope to hear from you and perhaps to have the pleasure of meeting you.

Sincerely,

Appendix 5-3

INITIAL LETTER
(Pitfalls)

Mr. Thomas Jones
123 Rolling Hills Drive
Zenith, Wisconsin

Dear Mr. Jones:

It has come to my attention that you may well possess material that is important to my library, and therefore I have decided to ask that you place the material where it will serve others, by effectively producing serious studies that will contribute to a national picture of the natural history field.

Our library is active in collecting materials of this nature, and without question is the most important in the nation. I expect a good many other collections to support those already in our possession. I have, for example, one collection which relates to Smith Creek. I have an effective public relations program seeking donations to our unique library.

I make all our collections available to anyone with any purpose in mind, and produce unlimited microfilms and photocopies in order to provide free access to all records.

I plan to call upon you soon to show you the glossy photographs of my library and some of the outstanding collections that I am proud to possess.

Very truly yours,

P.S. We also collect old typewriters, bookends, stationery (even the verso of used paper makes good scratch paper), books, magazines, tables, and chairs.

Appendix 5-4

SECOND LETTER
(A reminder that the library has received no response)

Dr. Thomas Jones
123 Rolling Hills Drive
Zenith, Wisconsin

Dear Dr. Jones:

A few weeks ago we wrote you about our interest in building a collection of original source materials to support study in our public library. The collection focuses on regional natural history, with special emphasis on records such as diaries, letters, field notes, and publications.

We would like to reassure you of the interest of our library, and hope that you will respond to the suggestion contained in our earlier letter.

Sincerely,

Appendix 6

FIELD NOTES

Originator: _____   Date: _____

Type, size and location:

    Manuscript materials _____

    Books _____

    Other _____

Importance:

Availability:

Contact: name   _____

                  address _____

                  phone   _____

Potential collections not previously known:

    Manuscript materials _____

    Books _____

    Other _____

Send: Library publication

             Supporting letter from academic department

             Inventory of similar collection

             Confirming letter to emphasize

Stipulations:	Disposal	Appraisal
	Restrictions	Book plates
	Available to family	Other

Other leads:	Similar vocation	Friends
	Relatives	Neighbors

Appendix 7-1

SAMPLE RECEIPT OF GIFT

To:

The _____ Library wishes to acknowledge with sincere appreciation the items listed below. This collection will be retained by the _____
_____ Library in _____ to be organized and preserved according to
customary library practice, though the donor authorizes the Library to dispose of any items determined to have insufficient research value to warrant
permanent retention.

Received:

Received on behalf of the _____
Library by: _____
_____

_____
Donor
_____
Date

Appendix 7-2

SAMPLE DEED OF GIFT
(Musician and/or composer)

I hereby give and bequeath to the _____ Library, at _____,
to be part of the _____ Library, at _____, the following described
material:

> Correspondence, music manuscripts, published pieces and
> miscellaneous items of _____.

The collection of materials is to be known as the _____ Collection,
and is to be arranged, inventoried, and indexed in the style and manner usual
in library practice.

The Collection is to be available for research purposes, with the following
provisos:

> 1. Performance and literary rights to the collection shall reside
>   with the donor or with persons he/she may designate, for a
>   period of _____ years, after which literary and performance
>   rights shall reside with the _____ Library.

2. In cases where performance and literary rights to material in the collection are not controlled by the donor, the Library shall exercise care, so that no publication of manuscripts is made without permission from the writer, composer, musicians, or their heirs.

3. No reproduction of the collection as a whole on microfilm, or other microform, shall be made without permission from the donor, so long as the literary and performance rights to the collection reside with the donor.

4. The _____ Library undertakes to use its best efforts to prevent plagiarism of the _____ material in any form.

5. The entire collection or any part thereof will be placed under seal for _____ years. This precludes any access to the material for any purpose for the duration of the period of closure of the collection.

Signed _____

Date _____

_____

For the Library

Appendix 7-3

SAMPLE DEED OF GIFT

I hereby give to the _____ Library at _____ to be part of the
_____ Library at _____ , the following described materials:

> The papers of _____ including letters, manuscripts, docu-
> ments, pamphlets, photographs, maps, and miscellaneous records,
> inclusive dates.

The collection of materials is to be known as the _____ Collection,
and is to be arranged, inventoried, and indexed in the style and manner usual
in the library practice.

The collection is to be available for research purposes, with the following
provisos:

1. Rights to the collection shall reside with the donor or with
   persons he may designate during his lifetime, after which
   rights shall reside with the _____ Library.

2. In cases where rights to material in the collection are not controlled by the donor, the library shall exercise care, so that no publication of manuscripts is made without permission from the writers or their heirs.

3. No reproduction of the collection as a whole on microfilm or other microform shall be made without permission from the donor, so long as the rights to the collection reside with the donor.

Signed _____

Date _____

_____

For the Library

Appendix 7-4

BOX IDENTIFICATION LABEL

NAME	NEW COLLECTION/ADDENDA
DATE RECEIVED	
ORGANIZER	MODEL
REMARKS	
APPRAISAL NEEDED YES/NO	NO. OF CARTON _____ NO. IN SERIES _____

Appendix 7-5

PROGRESS OF MANUSCRIPT ARRANGEMENT FORM

The collection of ____creator's name____

    DONOR _____

        Address _____

IN PROCESS

    Date coll. received _____ ( ); where stored _____ ( )

        date organized, where stored _____ ( ); call no. _____

    Biographical data; date requested _____ ( ); date

        received _____ ( ); Introduction written _____ ( ).

    Inventory xeroxed, no. of copies _____ ( ).

    Disposition of associated library:

	Books	Periodicals	Pamphlets	Journals
added				
discarded				
exchanged				
book sale				

APPRAISAL:

Appraiser_____; date appraisal requested _____ ( );

date received _____ ( ); tax year 19____ ; appraised

value _____ ; gift slip _____ ( ); report of gift sent

_____ ( ).

SENT TO DONOR

Acknowledgement _____ ( ); Inventory _____ ( );

Appraisal_____ ( ).

PRESS RELEASE

Written, filed _____ ( );

Sent to News Bureau, via office _____ ( );

Published (date, publication) _____ .

( ) please initial

Appendix 7-6

COLLECTION INVENTORY SAMPLE

William Carlson Smith Inventory

University of Oregon Library, September 1967

Introduction

William Carlson Smith graduated in 1907 from Grand Island College, Grand
Island, Nebraska, having majored in arts and letters. In his early career, Smith
held various positions: high school principal, teacher, Red Cross worker, field
worker and probation officer. Unfortunately the correspondence and related
materials pertaining to this period are not included in this collection, which
consists of materials dating from 1912. Dr. Smith did educational work in
Assam, India, under the American Baptist Foreign Mission Society from 1912-
1915. This collection includes notebooks, sketches, and correspondence concerning India as the Smiths found it, as well as manuscript materials which
resulted in Smith's first major work, *The Ao Naga Tribe of Assam*.

Following his return to this country Smith continued his studies at the University of Southern California and the University of Chicago majoring in sociology. Since 1920 he has held positions in the Sociology Departments of various universities.

During his tenure at Texas Christian University, 1929-1933, Smith became actively involved in a drive for investigation of the administration policies by the American Association of University Professors. Smith and his followers charged that nepotism and favoritism combined with poor management of funds to the extent that faculty members had no security in their jobs and were often dismissed without cause. The correspondence and reports concerning these investigations are included in this collection.

Perhaps Smith's most important work was *The Stepchild* which, when published in 1953, was the culmination of fifteen years of research and study. As the first definitive work on the subject it was widely acclaimed. This collection contains a large section of manuscript materials related to *The Stepchild*. Much of the research was done in Oregon while Smith was at Linfield College.

Other fields of interest investigated by Smith were immigration and second-generation Orientals in America. These interests are reflected in a number of articles by Smith which are included in the collection.

The William Carlson Smith collection consists largely of correspondence, manuscripts, related materials, and publications.

Note: Appendix 7-6 continued on following page.

William Carlson Smith Inventory

University of Oregon Library, September 1967

I.   Incoming Correspondence

re: *Americans in the Making.* 4 letters. 1939.
re: *Ao Naga Tribe of Assam.* 9 letters. 1926-1933.
D. Appleton-Century Company. 68 letters. 1937-1950.
Ashburn, Karl E. (Economist, associated with the T.C.U. investigation). 9 letters. 1933.
Bell, Vera. (former student, social worker). 5 letters. 1931.
Cameron, E. C. (Theologian, associated with the T.C.U. investigation). 8 letters. 1933.
Cissman, Martha. (former student). 14 letters. 1942-1949.
Clark, Carroll D. (Sociologist, University of Kansas). 5 letters. 1937.
Curry, Arthur R. (former member of T.C.U. faculty). 11 letters. 1933.
Dahlby, Albert. 3 letters, 2pp. biographical sketch, 2 letters of recommendation, 1 photo. 1936-1939.
Dana, Marshall. (Editor *Oregon Journal*, Chairman of Board of Trustees, Linfield College. Letters concern accusations that Smith was pro-German). 6 letters. 1942.
Derwacter, Frederick M. (Professor of Greek and Registrar of William Jewell College). 4 letters. 1937-1954.
Dodge, Homer L. (Dean of Graduate School, University of Oklahoma; Field Director, A.A.U.P. Committee on College and University Teaching). 7 letters. 1931-1933.
Duncan, H.G. (Sociologist). 11 letters. 1929-1933.
Family. 19 letters. 1914-1952.
Faris, Ellsworth. (Sociologist at University of Chicago). 18 letters. 1921-1951.
Fenter, M. H. 6 letters. 1930-1931.
Fishbein, Morris. (Physician, author, editor). 12 letters. 1946-1955.
Francis, James A. (Baptist minister). 8 letters. 1917-1927.
Francis, Roy. (Sociologist). 23 letters. 1946-1952.
Gebauer, Paul. 5 letters. 1943-1961.
Gettys, W. E. (Sociologist). 6 letters. 1929-1930.
Giltner, John. 6 letters. 1946-1950.
Glaze, J. A. (Associated with the T.C.U. investigation). 8 letters. 1931-1933.

Incoming Correspondence (cont'd)

    Griffing, Lamar. (former student). 9 letters. 1930-1933.

    Gustafson, C. V. (Sociologist at Lewis and Clark College).
       11 letters. 1948-1954.

    Higgins, L. R. (Professor of Greek). 9 letters. 1912-1951.

    Hintz, August M. (Baptist minister). 4 letters. 1938-1945.

    Horak, Jacob. (Sociologist). 5 letters. 1927-1939.

    Huzar, Elias. (Sociologist). 37 letters. 1935-1947.

. . . . .

[omitted page continues with the alphabetical arrangement]

William Carlson Smith, page 3

    Unidentified Incoming Correspondence. 12 letters. 1913-1960.

II.   Outgoing Correspondence

    re: *Americans in the Making.* 13 letters. 1927-1946.

    re: *The Ao Naga Tribe of Assam.* 6 letters. 1921-1933.

    D. Appleton-Century. 65 letters. 1918-1927.

    Baptist Church. 17 letters. 1918-1927.

    Bell, Vera. 5 letters. 1931-1932.

    Cameron, E. C. 6 letters. 1933.

    Cissman, Martha. 6 letters. 1943-1949.

    Curry, Arthur R. 9 letters. 1933.

    Duncan, H. G. 10 letters. 1929.

    Elmer, M. C. 5 letters. 1929-1939.

    Family. 16 letters. 1918-1960.

    Faris, Ellsworth. 22 letters. 1921-1939.

    Fenter, M. H. 7 letters. 1931.

    Fishbein, Morris. 9 letters. 1946-1955.

    Francis, Roy. 13 letters. 1933-1952.

    Gettys, W. E. 6 letters. 1929-1934.

    Glaze, J. A. 17 letters. 1931-1933.

    Grants:

        American Association for the Advancement of Science. 1 letter.
           1938.

        Missouri Academy of Science. 3 letters. 1937.

        Social Science Research Council. 27 letters. 1937-1953.

Outgoing Correspondence (cont'd)

Griffing, Lamar. 10 letters. 1930-1934.

Higgins, L. R. 5 letters. 1928-1951.

Horak, Jacob. 5 letters. 1927-1939.

Hutton, J. H. 5 letters. 1926-1938.

Huzar, Elias. 12 letters. 1935-1948.

India letters:

10 letters of Enid S. Smith. 1912-1914.

8 sketches by William C. Smith.

University of Kansas. 6 letters. 1930-1937.

Keck, Leander and Elinor. 4 letters. 1949-1954.

Kirk, William. 5 letters. 1929-1940.

Knox, Walter S. 10 letters. 1933-1934.

Larsell, Olof. 5 letters. 1941-1946.

Leftwich, Lacey Lee. 22 letters. 1930-1953.

Linfield College. 21 letters. 1937.

Manley, Charles. 24 letters. 1944-1955.

Mills, J. P. 8 letters. 1925-1938.

Pi Gamma Mu. 5 letters. 1934-1937.

Pihlblad, Carl T. 8 letters. 1931-1950.

Presbyterian Ministers' Fund for Life Insurance. 5 letters. 1933.

Rainwater, Clarence E. 4 letters. 1921.

Rosenquist, Carl M. 6 letters. 1931-1949.

Ross, Edward A. 15 letters. 1937-1939.

re: *Second Generation Orientals in America.* 11 letters. 1927-1937.

Shideler, Ernest H. 6 letters. 1929-1933.

Small, Albion W. 6 letters. 1922-1925.

Starr, Frederick. 5 letters. 1922-1923.

re: *The Stepchild.* 44 letters. 1936-1954.

Taylor, Luther R. 5 letters. 1946-1954.

Territorial Normal School, Honolulu, Hawaii. 6 letters. 1927-1930.

Texas Christian University Investigations, 1931-1934.

American Association of University Professors. (H.W. Tyler). 11 letters. 1931-1933.

Dodge, Homer. (A.A.U.P. Field Directory). 5 letters. 1931-1933. (Also includes Report of the investigation).

Hall, Colby D. (Dean T.C.U.). 5 letters. 1929-1932.

Scurlock, Nelson L. (Attorney). 2 letters. 1933-1934.

Outgoing Correspondence (cont'd)

T.C.U. Business Office. 6 letters. 1929-1930.

Waits, E. M. (President of T.C.U.). 7 letters. 1929-1933.

Miscellaneous letters. 11 letters. 1929-1934.

Thomas, W. I. 7 letters. 1926-1927.

Tuttle, Thomas H. 21 letters. 1928-1952.

Vanport Extension Center, O.S.S.H.E. (Stephen Epler). 8 letters. 1946-1947.

Watson, Walter T. 6 letters. 1930-1940.

William Jewell College. 5 letters. 1933-1952.

General Outgoing Correspondence

A-E. 63 letters. 1924-1961.

F-J. 52 letters. 1923-1960.

K-P. 54 letters. 1924-1954.

Q-Z. 64 letters. 1923-1961.

Unidentified (first names only). 4 letters. 1939-1955.

III. Manuscripts [fl.=folder]

A. Books

Americans in Process. Ann Arbor, Mich., Edwards Brothers, 1937. reviews and advertisements. 1 fl.

Americans in the Making. New York, D. Appleton-Century, 1939.

galley proofs

page proofs (incomplete)

miscellaneous 1 fl.

notes and fragments

copies of reviews

dust jacket

biographical sketch of Edward Alsworth Ross, (editor).

notes and fragments on immigration

The Ao Naga Tribe of Assam. London, Macmillan, 1925.

research notes

page proofs

copies of reviews

Manuscripts (cont'd)

> *The Stepchild.* Chicago, University of Chicago Press, 1953.
>> research notes (including part of 1st draft)
>> carbon
>> galley proofs
>> page proofs
>> acknowledgements (rought draft)
>> revised pages 200-201
>> biographical information about Smith
>> advertisement
>> correspondence securing permission to quote various sources

> B. Chapters from Books
>> "Communication" (original title "Communication and Its Social Significance"). Chapter 13 in a book by Pendell.
>>> carbon with pencil corrections
>>> galley proofs with corrections
>> "Indices of Social Disorganization". Chapter XVIII of *An Introduction to Sociology.*
>>> page proofs
>> "The Process of Social Disorganization". Chapter XIX of *An Introduction to Sociology.*
>>> page proofs

> C. Speeches and Articles
>> "Divorce in Oregon" Speech given at the meeting of the Northern Division (not further identified)
>>> abstract (published form)
>>> notes
>> "Divorce Trends in Missouri"
>>> holograph
>>> carbon
>> "Gaps in Our Knowledge Relative to Racial and Cultural Factors in Japanese-American Inter-Action" Prepared for the Social Science Research Conference, March 21-23, 1940.
>>> original
>>> carbon
>> "Genesis of Race Attitudes" Criticism of Carroll Clark's paper with the same title. Presented before the Southwestern Social Science Association, Dallas, Texas, March 30, 1934.
>>> carbon
>>> copy of Clark's paper

Manuscripts (cont'd)

"The Hybrid in Hawaii As a Marginal Man" *American Journal of Sociology*. vol. XXXIX, no. 4, Jan. 1934, pp. 459-468.
research notes
2 drafts
copy of published article
"India and Ghandi"
carbon
"The Life History Theme in English Classes" *Hawaii Educational Review*. March 1927.
carbon
"Personality Types"
carbon
"Problems of Rural Churches"
original
"The Social Sciences in an Integrated Curriculum" Presented to the Dana College Chapter of the A.A.U.P., May 2, 1960.
mimeograph
correspondence relative to Ph.D. programs
"Sociologists, What Now?" Prepared as the Presidential Address for the annual meeting of the Pacific Sociological Society. Reprinted in *Research Studies of the State College of Washington*, vol. XIII, no. 1, March, 1945, pp. 3-10.
2 versions
published copy
"Status and the Marginal Man"
research fragments
2 versions
bibliography

D. Published Articles without Manuscripts
"Changing Personality Traits of Second Generation Orientals in America" Reprinted from *The American Journal of Sociology*, vol. XXXIII, no. 6, May 1928.
"Difficulties of the Small Sociology Department" Reprinted from *Sociology and Social Research*, vol. 35, no. 4, March-April, 1951.
"The Ethnological Approach to the Family" *Journal of Applied Sociology*, vol. VIII, no. 2, Nov.-Dec., 1923.
"Minority Groups in Hawaii" Reprinted from *The Annals of The American Academy of Political and Social Science*, Sept., 1942.
"Missionary Activities and the Acculturation of Backward Peoples" *Journal of Applied Sociology*, vol. VII, no. 4, March-April, 1923.

Manuscripts (cont'd)

"Occupational Attitudes and the Minister" *Pastoral Psychology*, vol. 14, no. 133, April, 1963.

"Racial Prejudice to Be Lessened If Merit Is Seen" *Japanese-American Courier*, January 1, 1930.

"The Rural Mind: A Study in Occupational Attitude" Reprinted from *The Journal of Sociology*, vol. XXXII, no. 5, March, 1927.

"The Second Generation Oriental-American" *Journal of Applied Sociology*, vol. X, no. 2, Nov.-Dec., 1925.

"Some Problems in Sociological Research" *The Mid-Pacific Magazine*, vol. XXXV, no. 4, April, 1928.

"The Stepchild" Reprinted from *American Sociological Review*, vol. X, no. 2, April, 1945.

"When Will the Churches Wake Up?" Reprinted from *The Journal of Religious Thought*, vol. XIX, no. 1, 1962-1963.

"Why Fear Ideas?" Reprinted from *The Personalist*, vol. 42, no. 2, Spring, 1961.

"The 'Yes Man' on the Campus" Reprinted from *The Educational Forum*, May, 1960.

"The Young People of Hawaii" *Svenska Standaret*, Jan. 28, 1930.

E. Book Reviews

Hughes, Everett Cherrington, and Helen MacGill Hughes, *Where Peoples Meet: Racial and Ethnic Frontiers*. Glencoe, Illinois, The Free Press, 1952.
        carbon

Moon, Penderel *Strangers in India*, New York, Reynal and Hitchcock, 1945.
        carbon

Vedder, Clyde B. *The Juvenile Offender: Perspectives and Readings*, Garden City, New York, Doubleday, 1954.
        carbon

F. Manuscripts by Other Authors

Myrick, Lockwood, Jr., "An Open Letter to Honorable Wallace R. Farrington on Fukanga's Insanity."
        carbon

Noss, Theodore K., "Coordinating a Varied Teaching Program with Research"
        carbon

Rainwater, Clarence E., "Play as Collective Behavior"
        carbon

Manuscripts (cont'd)

        Reuter, E. B., "The Social Process"
        carbon

    G. Miscellaneous
       Second Generation Orientals in America
          research notes and fragments probably used in more than
          one publication. 8 fl.
       Notes on war 1 fl.
       Unidentified notes and fragments 1 fl.
       Course Outlines 1 fl.
       Indian Language Studies
          7 Indian Exercise Books
          5 papers
       Illustrated Lecture on "The Naga Tribes of India"
          narrative notes
       T.C.U. Departmental Reports and Recommendations
          Sociology Department, 1931-1934
       History of the Wilton Center Baptist Church
       Proceedings of the Committee for Uniting the Wilton Churches,
          1918.
       Constitution for the Faculty of Olivet College
       Court Transcript relating to the citizenship of a Hindu man.
          Smith testified for the defense, stating that Hindus
          were Caucasians
       "Grumble" (apparently a senior class speech)
       Anti-Japanese materials 1 fl.
       Linn-County Fire Patrol Association
          minutes and correspondence. 1946-1952.
       Oregon Prison Association
          minutes and correspondence 1946-1953.
       William C. Smith Credentials 1 fl.
          letters of recommendation
          college transcripts, etc.
          clippings
          Miscellaneous photographs 1 fl.
          16 diaries and notebooks. (Some written in India
            describing social conditions, climate, economy,
            etc. 1912-1914)
          1 geometry notebook
          1 ledger
          1 autograph book
          1 box of notes on Indonesia written during 1926-1927

Appendix 7-7

COLLECTION INVENTORY SAMPLE

Lowell Brentano
and
Frances Hyams Brentano
Collection
University of Oregon Library
July 1970

An article on Lowell Brentano in the *New York World* of February 17, 1929, headlines him as "A publisher by day, a playwright by night," and opens, "Something, there seems to be, in American atmosphere conducive to the hyphen in careers." As the years passed, Brentano continued to hyphenate new phases to his career, a Burbank of belles lettres, until he was Lowell Brentano, publisher-playwright-novelist-editor-screenwriter-publishers, scout-literary agent-magazine writer-collaborator.

After graduating with honors from Harvard in 1918, Brentano joined the family firm in an editorial capacity, later becoming first vice-president, splitting his time between the retail operation and publishing. All the while, evenings and Sundays, Brentano was writing plays. His interest in theater began early, "Coming across from Orange, N.J. to go on a playgoing orgy." At Harvard, he took courses in dramatic history and was associated with the "47 Workshop." In 1926, he authored, with Fulton Oursler, a play, "The Spider," which enjoyed a long New York run, translation and performance in seven European countries, and performance in London. Other Brentano plays include "Zeppelin," written with McElbert Moore and Earle Crooker, "Family Affairs," and "Danger—Men Working," authored with Ellery Queen. Mr. Brentano split writing responsibilities with Earle Crooker and Frederick Loewe (of Lerner and Loewe) for a musical, "Great Lady."

Frances Hyams received her Ph.D. in English from Radcliffe in 1917. While studying there, she was an active member of the "47 Workshop" group. After teaching a semester at Wellesley, she married Lowell Brentano, whom she had met in the Workshop. She became editor of "Brentano's Book Chat," developing it from a house organ into "A magazine of distinction and literary controversy." As the publishing arm of Brentano's expanded, she gave up "Book Chat" for editorial work and literary scouting. She brought the Harvard Play Series and the early works of birth control pioneer Margaret Sanger to Brentano's.

In 1933, the Brentanos left the family business and concentrated on their writing careers. Mr. Brentano wrote original material for movies, more plays, magazine articles and a novel, *The Melody Lingers On*, which was made into a movie. A story he wrote in conjunction with Stuart Palmer, "The Penguin Pool Murders," also became a movie.

Mrs. Brentano aided her husband critically and editorially and wrote magazine articles and fiction during the thirties and forties. Immediately following World War II, collaborating with Halford Luccock of Yale Divinity School, she edited a religious anthology entitled *The Questing Spirit*.

While Mrs. Brentano and Luccock were assembling the anthology, the following appears in an undated letter from him:

> I have not looked over Eliot's "Murder in the Cathedral"
> for our purpose. Will do so. It is the best known religious
> drama of recent years (I can hear Lowell hiss "Closet
> drama") but sometimes good stuff is stored away in closets.

After the release of *The Questing Spirit*, Mrs. Brentano embarked on a new project, an anthology on *The Big Cats*. A third collection, *The Word Lives On*, was published in 1951.

Volta Review, June, 1941, contains a Brentano article, "S.O.S. for Doctors." This appears to be the first of many articles on hearing which he wrote. A book, *Ways to Better Hearing*, was published in 1945.

The Brentano collection includes extensive correspondence with Fulton Oursler, who, after becoming editor of *Liberty Magazine* in 1931, left the business end of their collaborative efforts in the hands of Mr. Brentano. Two brief letters on this subject seem to epitomize the relationship of the two men.

April 30, 1931

Mr. Lowell Brentano
Brentano's Publishing
27th St. and 5th Ave.
New York, New York.

Dear Lowell:

Jesus, Mary and Joseph! Why aren't the amateur rights of *The Spider* sold?

Piously yours,
/s/ Fulton

May 4, 1931

Fulton Oursler
217 W. 70th St.
New York, New York.

Dear Fulton:

By the law of the Medes, Persians and Moses, between Samuel French on one hand, and McCarthy and Sam Harris on the other, what can one poor lone Jew do to sell the amateur rights of *The Spider*?

Fervently yours,
/s/ Lowell Brentano

Other Brentano correspondents include George Bernard Shaw, George Moore, Lord Dunsany and John Benn of the English publishing house, Ernest Benn, Limited from Great Britain. His American letters include Jerry Wald, who was, during the period of their most frequent correspondence, a contract writer, J. Frank Dobie, and James Geller, then with the William Morris Agency. Single letters include Anita Loos, Jean Sibelius and Per Hallstrom.

There are twenty-three play manuscripts in the collection, written either singly by Mr. Brentano, or in collaboration with other writers. One of particular interest is "Torches in the Night," a musical about Currier and Ives. Mr. Brentano wrote in a form peculiar to screen writers in the ten Extended Screen Treatments in the collection. They appear to be a scenario extended to novelette length.

Lowell Brentano died July 8, 1950. From that time until this collection ends, in 1953, Mrs. Brentano continued his activities with the New York League for the Hard of Hearing and as publishing scout for several major publishers.

Lowell Brentano
and
Frances Hyams Brentano
Collection
University of Oregon Library
July 1970
Preliminary Inventory

Correspondence

Incoming. 1917-1952. 1932

A.

Abbott, George. 1937, 1948. 2
Abingdon-Cokesbury Press. 1949. 1
Alger and Coughlin. 1927. 1
Aldrich, Bess Streeter. 1950. 3
George Allen and Unwin Ltd. 1950-1952. 8
The American Dramatists. 1927-1937. 13
American Industrial Bankers Association. 1940. 1
The American Mercury Magazine. 1947. 1
The American Museum of Natural History. 1946. 4
American Play Company. 1927-1932. 6
D. Appleton Century. 1947-1950. 5
Archibald, S. G. 1950, 1952. 2
Arliss, Mike. 1929. 1
Armbruster, Dorothy. 1949-1952. 24
Art and Educational Publishers Ltd. 1948. 1
Aster, N. 1931-1932. 4
The Atlantic Monthly. 1946. 2
Auden, W. H. Undated. 1
The Author's League of America. 1935-1942. 6

B.

Bank of New York and Fifth Avenue Bank. 1951. 1
Batchelder, Roger. 1939. 1
Beals, Carleton. 1930. 1
Bender, James F. 1950-1951. 4

Correspondence, Incoming, (cont'd)

Ernest Benn Limited. 1946-1950. 56
Berg, Louis. 1934. 1
Phil Berg–Bert Allenberg Inc. 1942. 1
Bethune-Cookman College. 1951. 1
Bickerton, Joseph P. Jr. 1929-1931. 12
Bigbee, North. 1933. 1
Blackall, Dorothy B. 1937. 1
Blankfort, Henry. Undated. 3
Blau, Bela. 1929. 1

. . . . .

[omitted pages continue the alphabetically arranged incoming correspondence]

12. Brentano Inventory

Correspondence, Incoming. (cont'd)

W.

Wooden, W. H. 1940. 1
Woodhouse, Henry. 1931. 2
Woods, Edward. 1949. 1
Works Progress Administration. Federal Theater Project.
1936-1937. 20
World Book Company. 1946. 2
World Calender Association. 1952. 2
The World's Work (1913) Limited. 1947. 2
Wornum, Miriam. 1948-1951. 11

Y.

Yale University Press. 1948. 1
Your Life. 1939, 1946. 2

Z.

Zara, Louis. 1946, 1947. 2
Ziff-Davis Publishing Company. 1946-1951. 49
Zimmerman, Sara E. 1951. 1
Zuckerman. William. 1946. 1
Zung, Cecilia Sieu-ling, 1939. 1

Unsigned Correspondence. 13.

Correspondence, Outgoing. 1926-1952. Approximately 2450

Manuscripts.

   As Lowell Brentano was author and playwright, publisher, collaborator, publishing company scout and literary agent, it is difficult to ascertain what function he fulfilled in relation to these manuscripts. The title page listing is used here, but comparison with the contract and agreement folders would provide more complete information.

   Book Length.

      Four hundred phantoms. By Isadore Lhevinne. Carbon with holograph and editorial revisions. Pages 3 and 4 and 143-145 missing. 146p.

   Play. Date indicated is copyright date.

      Anything to please. By Russell Medcraft and Sheridan Gibney. "Suggested by Arthur Weigall's novel entitled 'Infidelity.' " Carbon. 109p.

      The badger. By LB. Carbon. Act I, Scene I missing. 108p.

      The beetle. Also titled "The Commissioner of Police." By Fulton Oursler and LB. Carbon. 98p.

      Between covers. By William Jourdan Rapp and LB. "Original Script." Carbon with holograph revisions. 119p.
      Revised version. Carbon. 196p.

      Danger—men working. By Ellery Queen and LB. Carbon. 164p.

      Encore. By Maurice A. Hanline, Lewis E. Gensler and LB. Carbon. 100p. Mimeograph. 102p.

      Family affairs. By LB. Carbon. 105p.

      The frozen web. By LB and Will Oursler. 1948. Carbon. 121p.

Manuscripts, Play. (cont'd)

> Great lady. Book by Earle Crooker and LB. Lyrics by Earle Crooker.
> Music by Frederick Loewe. Carbon. 173p.
> Holograph notes. 7p.

> When Greek meets girl. "Second act outline." 13p.
> First act only. Carbon. 98p.

> Loot. By Earle Crooker and LB. Carbon. 117p.

> Mistress. By Fulton Oursler and LB. 1930. Carbon. Incomplete.
> 47p.

> Now-a-days. By Fulton Oursler and LB. Carbon. 107p.

> Penguin Pool. Story by Fulton Oursler and LB. Novel by Stuart
> Palmer. Play by Tom Jones Leonard. 1931. Carbon. 136p.

> Queen Bee. By Lowell Brentano and Will Oursler. 1948. Carbon.
> 134p. Mimeograph. 103p.

> The police commissioner. By Fulton Oursler and LB. 1931.
> Carbon. 173p.

> Shelter. By William Jourdan Rapp and LB. Carbon 78p.
> Notes, memoranda and character studies. 74p.

> The spider. By Fulton Oursler and LB. 1926. "Original manuscript."
> Minor holograph revisions. 87p.
> "Acting copy." Carbon. With heavy production revisions. 103p.
> Technical stage instructions. 22p.

> Torches in the night. By Earle Crooker and LB. Carbon. 124p.
> List of music of the period of this musical. 7p.

> What you need in this world. By Martha Madison and LB.
> Carbon. 124p.

> The wildcat. By Lewis Waller and LB. 99p.

Manuscripts, Play. (cont'd)

The will to glory. By Jacque Le Clercq and LB. 112p.

Zeppelin. By McElbert Moore, Earle Crooker and LB. Carbon. 131p.

Extended Movie Treatments.

Call it art. By LB and Arch. Winick. Carbon. 71p.

Every girl for herself. By Clara Underhill and LB. Carbon. 96p.

Greek to you. By William Jourdan Rapp and LB. Carbon. 119p.
Synopsis. 8p.

Harbor police. Carbon. 69p.

Laughing gas. By LB and Arch. Winick. Carbon. 71p.

Music by mail. By Martha Madison and LB. Carbon. 62p.

Music in my heart. Carbon. 58p.

Night school. By LB and Jerry Wald. Carbon. 60p.

Smoke eater. By Jonathan Finn and LB. Carbon. 90p.

Tiger eyes. Carbon. 159p.

Movie Treatments and Synopses

By that sin fell the angels. From a novel by Judith Ravel and
LB. 9p.

China sea. By LB and Asa Bordages. 24p.

Dr. Kildare's naval secret. By LB and FHB. Carbon. 10p.

Flicker Alley. By Jerry Wald and LB. 44p.
Second version. Holograph revisions. 50p.

Manuscripts, Play. (cont'd)

Four hundred phantoms. By Isadore Lhevinne and LB. 3p.

Candid camera. Carbon. 12p.

Great lady. "A revised synopsis." By Earle Crooker and LB.
Carbon. 37p.

. . . . .

[omitted page 15 contains similar format and begins Manuscripts, Magazine Article]

16. Brentano Inventory

Manuscripts, Magazine Article. (cont'd)

The business of being a parent. By Dr. Ruth Conkey. Carbon. 19p.

Careers at home. Carbon. 4p.
Holograph notes. 2p.

Changed with the times. "Issued by the Committee of Education
and Public Information." The New York State Funeral Directors
and Embalmers Association, Inc. Carbon. 15p.

Cooperative living. By Benjamin and Sylvia Hyman and Ruth
Rubin. Carbon. 20p.

Divorce detectives. 14p.

Education for marriage. By FHB and LB. 15p.

Enough to live on. Carbon. 17p.

Financial democracy. Carbon. 21p.

Food magic for the army. Carbon. 14p.

Glamour girl with a badge. Carbon. 17p.

Hobbies for victory. Carbon. 14p.

Manuscripts, Magazine Articles, (cont'd)

Hockshop with a heart. Carbon. 11p.

This hospital business. Carbon. 30p.

How picture titles are made—and unmade. Carbon. 9p.

How to be a millionaire—and like it. Carbon. 18p.

How to be happy—though married. By John T. S. Wade as told to LB. 15p.

How to buy a used car safely. By Ralph Graeter and LB. Carbon. 13p.

I don't quite hear you. Carbon. 13p.

It ain't no sin. Carbon. 20p.

It does happen here. Carbon 22p.

I'm afraid to read the papers. By Mary Margaret McBride. Carbon. 5p.

Life is just a selling game. "Horatio Alger is wrong." Carbon. Holograph revisions. 21p.

. . . . .

[omitted pages employ same format]

20. Brentano Inventory

Notes, Research Material, Poetry and Selections for FHB Anthologies.

The Big Cats. 1 fl.

The Questing Spirit. 1 fl.
Speeches. 1 fl.

Publisher and Author Permissions for FHB Anthologies. 1 fl.

20. Brentano Inventory (cont'd)

Notes and Memoranda. 1 fl.

Theater Bills and Schedules. 1 fl.

Reviews. 1 fl.

Biographical Material.
  Lowell Brentano. 1 fl.
  Frances Hyams Brentano. 1 fl.

Memorabilia. 1 fl.

Books in Collection.

  Bride of a thousand cedars. By Bruce Lancaster and LB. New
    York. 1939. Stokes.

  By that sin fell the angels. By Judith Ravel and LB. New York.
    1935. Macauley.

  Personality Unlimited. By Veronica Dengel. LB Collaborator.
    Philadelphia. 1943. Winston.
    British Edition. London. 1949. Faber and Faber.

  Ways to better hearing. New York. 1946. Franklin Watts.

Scrapbook.

  The Questing Spirit.

Appendix 7-8

COLLECTION INVENTORY SAMPLE

Inventory of the Papers of James W. Clise

University of Oregon Library

April 1961

Introduction

In December 1960 James W. Clise made known his intention to place his correspondence files in the University of Oregon Library. Some months later these records became a permanent part of the University's collection concerned with our American heritage.

Mr. Clise corresponded regularly with the leaders of the American Conservative movement and his letters detail the philosophy which he and others developed in the post war period. Since Mr. Clise was a contributor of financial and philosophical assistance, his correspondence is vital to the student of the Conservative movement.

The collection is basically arranged in the manner that Mr. Clise had established. Thus the letters are arranged by the organization, association, or individual. Dates are included to make the files more useful.

I. Correspondence and Subject Files

Inventory includes general alphabet and specific files for major correspondents and subjects.

Ad on foreign policy for America. 1955.
Agrarian Reform. 1955.
Aid Refugee Chinese Intellectuals. 1952-1953.
American Bureau for Medical Aid to China. 1951-1961.
American China Policy Association. (Alfred Kohlberg). 1951-1954.
American Council of Christian Laymen. (Verne P. Kaub). 1957.
American Economic Foundation. General. 1949-1960.
_____. Pacific Northwest District. 1952-1954.
_____. Program in Latrobe, Pa. 1951-1952.
American Enterprise Association. 1958-1961.
American Farm Bureau Federation. 1955.
American Mercury. 1951-1957.
American Motors. (George Romney). 1957-1958.
Americans for Constitutional Action. (Ben Moreell). 1958-1959.
America's Future. (John T. Flynn). 1947-1960.
Andelson, Robert Vernon. (Arlington College). 1955-1957.
Anderson, Robert B. (U.S. Secretary of Treasury). 1959.
Andrews, Lloyd. (Washington State Superintendent of Schools).
    1956-1958.
Andrews, T. Coleman. 1958.
Anti-subversion laws. 1954.
Armstrong Cork Co. (H. W. Prentis, Jr.). 1956-1960.
Arnold, Lawrence. 1956-1958.
Asia Foundation. (Asia College). 1955-1956.
Association of Washington Industries. 1957-1961.
Automobile Club of Washington. 1949-1954.

Baker, Dorothy. 1957-1958.
Baker, Frederick E. 1944-1954.
Bank of America. 1952-1954.
Bannon, Thomas J. (Western Gear Works, Seattle). 1951-1952.
Bantz, William. 1958.
Barrie, Jay. 1958-1959.
Barron, Bryton: "Inside the State Department." 1957-1959.
Bayley, Frank S., Sr. 1952-1958.
Beezley, P. C. 1959.

Correspondence and Subject Files (cont'd)

       Better Business Standards Association. 1951.
       Bierly, Ivan R. (William Volker Fund). 1958-1959.
       John Birch Society. (Robert Welch). 1959-1960.
       Birnie, Helen W. 1956.
       Blum, Walter. 1957.
       Boggs bill. (H. R. 2815). 1956.
       Books. (Buying list). 1957-1959.

. . . . .

[omitted pages continue the alphabetical arrangement]

Clise Inventory—Page Seven

       Political. General. 1950-1959.
                   _____: Al Canwell for Congress Committee 1952.
                   _____: City. 1958-1960.
                   _____: Constitution Party. 1959-1960.
                   _____: Dear Bob. 1959.
                   _____: Fall campaigns. 1952-1958.
                   _____: King County. 1950-1958.
                   _____: National. 1950-1961.
                   _____: National. Washington State Congressmen. 1950.
                   _____: National. 1960 elections.
                   _____: National Presidential elections. 1952.
                   _____: "Questionnaire." 1960.
                   _____: Republican Campaign Committee of Washington.
                        1951-1954.
                   _____: State. 3 folders. 1950-1961.
                   _____: U. S. Congress. Walt Woodward Campaign. 1950.
       Pollock, David. Job Research, Inc. 1954-1960.
       Post Office Department. 1950-1960.
       Pound, Roscoe: "Legal Immunities of Labor Unions." 1957.
       Pro America. (National Organization of Republican Women). 1951-
          1955.
       Preferential voting. 1958.
       Project X. 1958.

       Railroad rates. 1958.
       Rainier Club. 1959.
       Reader's Digest, 1960-1961.

Clise Inventory—Page Seven (cont'd)

Henry Regnery Company. 1958.
Reinhardt, Bryson. 1956-1959.
R.O.T.C. Oath. 1955.
Richardson Foundation. 1957.
Robinson, Claude. (Opinion Research Corporation, Princeton Panel).
1957.
Rogge, Ben A. (Wabash College). 1958-1959.
Rottenberg, Simon. (University of Chicago). 1960.
Rowe, David N. (Yale University). 1957.
Russell, Dean. 1958-1960.
Russia and the Big Red Lie by Lloyd Mallon. 1959-1960.

SPX. (Tom R. Hutton). 1960-1961.
St.-Ivanyi, Alexander. 1958-1961.
Sample literature. 1948-1950.
"Say it safely" by Paul Ashley. 1957.
School directors project. 1954-1955.
Schoolmaster Case, by Jay Morrison. 1957-1958.
Schwarz, Fred C. 1957-1958.
Schweppe, Alfred J. 1955-1958.
Seattle Chamber of Commerce. 1959.
Seattle Foundation. 1949-1951.
Seattle Post Intelligencer editorial. 1950-1954.
Seattle Public Library. 1950-1956.
Seattle Symphony. 1950.
Silver. 1953.
Single tax. 1957-1958.

. . . . .

[omitted page continues the alphabetical arrangement]

Clise Inventory—Page Nine

Watts, V. Orval. 1957-1960.
Weeks, Sinclair. 1957.
Western Tax Council. 1960.
Westland, Jack, 1955-1958.

Clise Inventory—Page Nine (cont'd)

> White, Andrew Dixon: "Fiat money inflation in France." 1959.
> Whitworth College. 1954-1960.
> Williams, Jay: "A sensible budget." 1959.
> Williams, W. Walter. 1952-1954.
> Wire tapping law. 1954-1955.
> "Wolf pack is now after Senator Eastland," by G. W. Robnett. 1956.
> World Affairs Council. 1952-1954.
> World's Fair. 1959.

> Yale-in-China. (W. R. Wheeler). 1952-1960.
> _____: Fund raising campaign. 1948.
> Yale University. 1948-1957.
> _____: Scholarship holders. 1956.
> _____: Torch society. 1955.
> Yankus, Stanley Jr. 1958-1959.
> Young Americans for Freedom. 1960-1961.
> Young Men's Christian Association. 1958.

> Zonolite Company. 1951-1959.

II.   Personal and Business Files

> Asbestos Building Partnership. (George Baccrich). 1939-1951.
> Asbestos Supply Company of Seattle. 1932-1951.
> Celotex Corporation. (Regional corporations). 1948-1951.
> James Clise Fund. 1952.
> Letters to and from parents, 1935-1936.

III.   Clise Speeches, Articles, Published Letters, etc.

> Form letters.
> Letters to the editor.
> Misc. comments.
> Speeches.
> Writings.

Appendix 7-9

BIOGRAPHICAL INFORMATION FOR PREPARATION OF MANUSCRIPT INVENTORIES

Name _____ Date _____

Address _____

Place of birth _____ Birth date _____

Educational history

Marital status _____

Number of children _____

When did you commence writing for publication?

When and where was your work first published?

Additional biographical information and/or comments.

In which standard biographical or bibliographical source are you listed?

Under what pseudonym(s) do you write?

Appendix 8-1

NAME CARD

```
Snow, Mrs. Charles              Alpine, WI

     see

Garbonneau, T. V.
```

Appendix 8-2

GEOGRAPHICAL CARD
(Lead card)

```
1st letter __1-4-78_____        2nd letter ___3-2-78_____

                                 Alpine, WI _____
Living
(Deceased)  Garbonneau, T. V. (1901-1961)_____

Profession _fiction writer___   Source _corresp. of Brian Wynne_

Relation and
  letter to _daughter:  Mrs. Charles Snow_____

Address _____123 Main St._____

WWA _no_____
WWWA v.# _v. 4 (biog. over)_     Local WW _____
Phonebook Madison_____           LAP _____
Tel. No. _(212) 123-4567_____    Other _Contemporary Author 3 v. 45
City Directory _____   Ask _____
Professional Directory _____
Biography Index _no  1961_____
NY Times Obit __no_____
```

Appendix 8-3

COME-UP, TICKLER, OR REMINDER FILE, BASED ON A
CALENDAR ARRANGEMENT

July 1

    Send second letters to:

        Allen, John   Tucson, Ariz.
        Allenton, Mary   Phoenix, Ariz.

    Decision: (donor is to let library know of his decision)

        Baxter, Fred T.   Seattle

    Shipment: (donor has reported he will ship by this date)

        Elmo, Harry   Denver   16 cartons

    Visit: (potential donor plans to stop at library)

        Jones, James   Local (will be here sometime during
                                     the week)

Appendix 10-1

POLICY

Municipal Library Gift Policy

Music Collection

The Municipal Library has established a collection of original sources and associated materials to preserve and protect the musical heritage of the community. The Library has set up certain necessary guidelines in order to preserve only those records that it deems important and that are of a primary and/or secondary research nature. It cannot begin to house the lesser records of the community as an archival function, nor can it be expected to preserve or restore records that have deteriorated beyond normal library condition.

The Library will preserve as individual units such records as correspondence, financial accounts, manuscripts, recordings, tapes, promotional literature, and publications relating to the community, when the records have a validity unto themselves. It cannot accept the random or unassociated piece, nor work designed primarily for the amusement of its creator. The Library's purpose is to collect community musical heritage, not personal memorabilia.

Use, administration, service, and disposition of unwanted or duplicate materials in regard to the collection are placed in the formal charge of the library administrator and his appointed officer, chief curator of the music collection. These librarians are entrusted with control of use of the materials, and, unless agreed otherwise at the time of gift, all reproduction and publication rights to the material reside with the Library.

The chief curator of the music collection and the library administrator are directly responsible for the policy and interpretation of the collection.

Appendix 10-2

SOLICITATION LETTER TO A COMPOSER

Mr. Elmo Bernstein
1235 Hollywood Blvd.
Portland, Oregon

Dear Mr. Bernstein:

For fifteen years, the Municipal Library has had a music room and small staff serving a large public interested in serious music. During the last several years, our patrons have shown a new interest in local composers whose work has been recognized both here and throughout the state. We have been pleased to learn of this awakening interest, yet disappointed that we had only your published music to show our users.

In the last six months, we have come to the conclusion that no institution in our community has taken the initiative to preserve the significant records of our present and earlier composers and musicians. We feel that this is a serious oversight, and we hope to gather an in-depth collection of original scores, drafts, correspondence with performers and publishers, and similar basic records. Such files will be kept within the Library under the name of the person who created them so that the collection will maintain its individuality.

We feel that the serious student today and the scholar of the future will seek out such files in order to understand both the composer and his audience. We would like to talk with you about the possibility of placing your non-current files in our special music collection.

Sincerely,

Appendix 10-3

SOLICITATION LETTER TO A MUSICIAN

Mrs. Alpha B. Smith
987 Omega Avenue
Portland, Oregon

Dear Mrs. Smith:

Our music section has been collecting the original working files of some of the early conductors in our community. We have read both magazines and pamphlets that discuss your grandfather's early organization of a community band, which seems to have had a very active role in the community during the 1880s, and through the Spanish American War.

We are writing to you with the thought that you may have your grandfather's musical arrangements, posters, and similar records, or that you may know where these materials are stored. We know that it is difficult to believe that his files have survived for such a long period, but we hope that you may be aware of their existence.

Our music section already has a good many pieces that were composed about the time your grandfather was active, and we have some personal letters from a gentleman who wrote a piece commemorating the fiftieth anniversary of our city. We believe that your grandfather may have been the first person to conduct the piece.

We would like to meet you to discuss our desire to place Mr. John Jones's work in our permanent collection, where it would be treasured and shared with future generations. Perhaps when we meet, we can convey some of our enthusiasm for our collection and its potential uses.

Sincerely,

Appendix 10-4

SAMPLE PAGES OF A DETAILED INVENTORY

Inventory of the Papers of Hans Ewald Heller
University of Oregon Library 1967

Hans Ewald Heller (1894-1966) was a composer, pianist, writer, and critic.
He was born in Vienna and held doctorates from the universities of Vienna
and Prague. Much of his creative life was after World War I, when he was a
contemporary of Schoenberg, Berg, Krenek, Webern, and others. As writer
and critic he appeared in the *Wiener Zeitung*, the *Neues Wiener Journal*, and
other publications.

He composed a musical comedy, many short operas, symphonic works,
chamber music, and songs. He fled Vienna in 1938 and came to the United
States, where he taught, edited, created film music, did program work for the
United States Information Service, and became music director of Hearst
Metrotone News.

The Heller papers consist of original scores, published music, copies and
originals of articles, correspondence, and tapes. The early songs and orchestral

pieces were written prior to 1938. A quintet for clarinet, piano and strings, a cantata, and an overture were written later, in the United States.

The collection is arranged in four groups: I—Original compositions in manuscript; II—Published music; III—Scrapbooks and loose papers; IV—Tapes.

The collection was inventoried and identified by Edmund F. Soule, Music Librarian, University of Oregon.

Note: Inventory begins on page 186.

Inventory of the Hans Ewald Heller Papers

I. Manuscript compositions.

1. The Ballad of all women.
Score. 23p. Holograph, pencil in music manuscript book. Piece
for mixed chorus with two-piano accompaniment. Text: Alfred
Kreymbourg. Published. Dedicated. Piece totals 210 measures,
is dated "May 19, 1943" foot of p. 23. A reduction of orchestral
and choral piece.

2. Black and white, oder die Höllenmaschine. Oper in einem Akt
von Dr. Fritz Zaref.
Score. 91p. Holograph in ink on music paper. Piano vocal score.
Text by Dr. Fritz Zaref. Published. Dedicated. Includes rehearsal
notes and corrections in red and blue pencil. For synopsis of
plot, see *Jealousy.*

3. Carnival in New Orleans (Mardi Gras); an American overture.
Score. 54p. Holograph, ink on transparency. For full orchestra.
Published. Dated at foot of p. 54, "New York, May 14, 1940.
HE Heller."

4. Carnival in New Orleans (Mardi Gras); an American overture.
1940. Score 51p. Holograph, ink on score paper. For full
orchestra. Published. Slip on title page: "This composition
is from the rental library of Maxwell Weaner . . . " Rehearsal
marks in red pencil. Barlines ruled in pencil.

5. (Children's songs)
Score. 11p. Holograph, ink on music papers. For high voice
and piano. Published. Dedicated. Contents: Jahreskind; Wenn
ich sein Lachen höre; Kindeserwachen. Corrections and
rehearsal marks in pencil. English translations of first two
songs in pencil.

I. Manuscript compositions. (cont'd)

    6. Chöre.
       Score. 2v. Holograph, pencil on music paper. Choruses, unaccompanied, written on 4 staves. v.1, 8p., SSAA; v.2, 11p., SATB. Published. Dedicated. Title from double sheet of music paper, cover. Contents: Vor der Ernte; Winteranfang; Sommermittag; Durch Knospengrün; Die Königstochter; Rätsel; Gebet; Froher Sinn.

Etc.

. . . . .

[omitted pages employ same format]

Hans E. Heller Inventory—8 (cont'd)

    45. Zwei Gedichte von Dehmel.
       Score. (7)p. Holograph, ink on music paper. Songs for medium voice and piano. Published. Dedicated. Contents: Der Schwimmer; Verklärung. Corrections in ink and pencil.

II. Published music.

    1. Das Lied vom braven Kind; Shimmy aus der dreiaktigen Operetta, Der Liebling von London. Wien, 1924. Text von Felix Doermann. Score. 3p. pl. no. E.B.0030.

    2. Das Lied vom Tulli-mann; One-step aus der dreiaktigen Operetta, Der Liebling von London. Wien, 1924. Text von Felix Doermann. Score. 3p. pl. no. E.B.0029.

    3. Ode to our Women; a Ballad of Our Time. Cantata for mixed chorus. Music by H. E. Heller. Lyric by Alfred Kreymbourg. N.Y., 1944. Score. 24p. pl. no. 12277-23. Vocal score.

    4. Pastorale und Scherzo über das gleiche Thema von Hans Ewald Heller. Wien, 1936. Score. 69p. Universal-Edition no. 10789.

    5. Wandlungen; Variationen über ein eigenes Thema für Orchester. London, etc., 1937. Score. 77p. pl. no. J.W.2646.

III.   Scrapbooks and loose papers.

Five volumes and 11 folders, including programs, reviews, poems, letters. There are letters from Paul Emerich, Selma Lagerlöf, Erich Korngold. Two posters feature works by Heller. There is also a script of "Arne's Treasure."

IV.   Tapes.

1. Little Suite for Orchestra. Suite for clarinet and piano. 1 reel.

2. Quintet, clarinet, piano, strings. 1 reel.

Appendix 10-5

SAMPLE CURSORY INVENTORY

Jean Williams Collection

University of Oregon Library 1967

Introduction

Born in England in 1876, Miss Williams moved to Toronto, Canada. After graduating from the Royal Conservatory of Music of the University of Toronto, she returned to England and studied to be a concert pianist.

A broken wrist switched her career to voice and she returned to the University of Toronto where she taught voice and piano. She later taught in Cleveland and St. Louis before moving to Portland, Oregon in 1932.

Miss Williams was past president of the National Music Teachers Association and past president of Mu Phi Epsilon. She became nationally known as a composer of piano compositions.

Miss Nellie Tholen, with whom Miss Williams collaborated on two music teaching books, gave the University of Oregon Library the Williams Collection of approximately 120 music manuscripts in 1967.

Jean Williams Collection
University of Oregon Library 1967

1. Correspondence—Incoming
   J. Fischer & Bro. (music publisher) 1 fl.
   Schroeder & Gunther, Inc. (music publisher) 2 fl.
   Misc. publishers 1 fl.
   Misc. correspondence 1 fl.

2. Misc. clippings and publicity releases. 1 fl.

3. Publications
   Sheet music
       Christmas Music for Treble Voices
       Slumber Little One
   Article
       A Teacher Talks of Concerto Form

4. Misc. manuscripts
   Harmony Digest
   What Is Music?

5. Sheet music manuscripts 4 fl.
       Adeste Fideles (transcription)
       Allegro a la Tarantella
       Aria
       Baby Moon
       Bells
       Bolero for Two Pianos (3 versions)
       The Boys Are Marching
       Cherry Ripe
       Concertino for Piano and String Orchestra
       Concerto in A Minor
       Concerto in C Minor
       Concerto in F Major
       Crossing the Bar
       Dance Johnny! (2 versions)
       Dance of the Puppets
       Dance with Me Polka

Sheet music (cont'd)

Dance with Me (2 versions)
Danza Espagnole
Do You Sleep (2 versions)
The Doll's Wedding
Dresden China Figures (Minuet V)
Fife and Drum
Fireside Memories
Flying Leaf
Four Christmas Songs
Four O'Clock in the Morning
Fun in Chinatown
Gavotte—violin and piano
Gavotte in G Major
A Grandfather Clock (3 versions)
Happy Dreams (2 versions)
Heritage
The Hermit Thrush
In Far Places
In Old Algiers
Indian Lullaby
Indian Tale
Joy to the World (transcription)
Junior Concerto, No. 6
Junior Piano Concerto, No. 6
Junior Concerto in G Major (2 versions)
Liebestraum No. 3 (Franz Liszt; transcription by J.W.)
A Little Irish Donkey
Lord Christ the Carpenter
Lord, Thou Hast Been Our Dwelling Place
Lovely Senorita
Low Tide (2 versions)
A Mother Song
A Musical Snuff Box (3 versions)
A Negro Lullaby
Noel
The Old Spinet
A Painted Fan (2 versions)
A Paisley Shawl
Partita (2 versions)
La Pastourelle Pensif (2 versions)

Sheet music (cont'd)

Patriots Song
Polka (2 versions)
Prelude Funebre
Rain! Rain!
Resurrection
Ring Out Wild Bells
The Roaming Bumble Bee
Scherzo in A Minor
Scout March
Sicilienne
Silent Night (transcription)
Simple Simon
Sleep Holy Child
Slumber Song
Snow by Night (2 versions)
Soldiers down the Street
Sonatina in G
Star of My Heart
A Strange Port (2 versions)
Street Parade
Tango in C Minor
These Are They (2 versions)
This is Oregon
To a Winter Robin (2 versions)
A Toby Jug
Toccata (2 versions)
Train Time (3 versions)
Valse in D Minor
Valse—violin and piano
Valse Chanson
Le Vin et les Cloches
The Wind and the Waves
Wind Chimes and Lanterns (2 versions)
Wind in the Night
Winter Sleep (3 versions)
Youth Concerto
Zwei Canzonen aus dem Fiori Musicale

Jean Williams Collection (cont'd)

6. Misc. scores (2 fl. largely untitled)
   violin arrangements
   working scores

7. Six manuscript notebooks

BIBLIOGRAPHY

INTRODUCTION

Library Literature, v.1- . New York, H. W. Wilson, 1933- .

Powell, Lawrence Clark. *The Alchemy of Books, and Other Essays and Addresses on Books and Writers*. Los Angeles, W. Ritchie Press, 1954.

Powell, Lawrence Clark. *Books in My Baggage: Adventures in Reading and Collecting*. Cleveland, World Pub., 1960.

Powell, Lawrence Clark. *The Little Packages: Pages on Literature and Landscape from a Traveling Bookman's Life*. Cleveland, World Pub., 1964.

Powell, Lawrence Clark. *A Passion for Books*. Cleveland, World Pub., 1958.

Randall, David Anton. *Dukedom Large Enough*. New York, Random House, 1969.

Rosenbach, Abraham S. Wolf. *Books and Bidders: The Adventures of a Bibliophile*. Boston, Little, Brown, 1927.

Targ, William, ed. *Bouillabaisse for Bibliophiles*. Cleveland, World Pub., 1955.

Targ, William. *Carrousel for Bibliophiles*. New York, Philip C. Duschnes, 1947.

Thompson, Lawrence Sidney. *Books in Our Times: Essays*. Washington, Consortium Press, 1972.

Wynar, Bohdan S. *Library Acquisitions: A Classified Bibliographic Guide to the Literature and Reference Tools.* 2nd ed. Littleton, Colo. Libraries Unlimited, 1971.

CHAPTER 1
PLANNING A SOLICITATION PROGRAM

Ash, Lee, comp. *Subject Collections: A Guide to Special Book Collections and Subject Emphases as Reported by University, College, Public and Special Libraries and Museums in the United States and Canada.* 4th ed. New York, Bowker, 1974.

Bordin, Ruth Birgitta Anderson. *The Modern Manuscript Library.* New York, Scarecrow Press, 1966.

Brewer, Frances J. "Friends of the Library and Other Benefactors and Donors." *Library Trends* 9:453-65 (April 1961).

Brubaker, Robert L. "Manuscript Collections." *Library Trends* 13:226-53 (October 1964).

Byrd, Cecil K. "Collecting Collections." *Library Trends* 9:434-36 (April 1961).

Carter, Mary Duncan. *Building Library Collections.* 4th ed. Metuchen, N.J., Scarecrow Press, 1974.

Downs, Robert B. "Collecting Manuscripts: By Librarians." *Library Trends* 5:337-43 (January 1957).

Duckett, Kenneth W. *Modern Manuscripts: A Practical Manual for Their Management, Care, and Use.* Nashville, American Association for State and Local History, 1975.
Without question, the best book concerning the subject.

Goodspeed, Charles Eliot. *Yankee Bookseller; Being the Reminiscences of Charles E. Goodspeed.* Boston, Houghton, Mifflin, 1927.

Kane, Lucile M. "Manuscript Collecting." In: *In Support of Clio: Essays in Memory of Herbert A. Kellar.* edited by William B. Hesseltine. Madison, State Historical Society of Wisconsin, 1958. pp. 29-48.

Lytle, Richard H., ed. "Management of Archives and Manuscript Collections for Librarians." *Drexel Library Quarterly* 11, no. 1 (January 1975). Collection of essays with two articles on the establishment and scope of manuscript collections.

Mearns, David C. "Historical Manuscripts, Including Personal Papers."
Library Trends 5:313-29 (January 1957).

Munby, Alan Noel Latimer. *The Cult of the Autograph Letter in England.*
London, University of London, Athlone Press, 1962.

National Union Catalog of Manuscript Collections. Washington, Library of
Congress, 1959/60- . Annual.
Commonly known as NUCMC, it publishes those holdings of manuscript collections reported by institutions willing to submit information; NUCMC does not include reports of material considered too
meager or unimportant.

Skelley, Grant T. "Characteristics of Collections Added to American Research
Libraries, 1940-1970: A Preliminary Investigation." *College and Research
Libraries* 36:53-60 (June 1975).

U.S. National Historical Publications Commissions. *A Guide to Archives and
Manuscripts in the United States.* Philip M. Hamer, ed. New Haven,
Yale University Press, 1961.
Commonly called "Hamer."

CHAPTER 2
POTENTIAL COLLECTION SPECIALTIES

Angle, Paul M. "The University Library and Its Manuscripts: An Excursion
into Other People's Business." *Library Quarterly* 15:123-30 (April 1945).

Brewer, Reginald. *The Delightful Diversion: The Whys and Wherefores of
Book Collecting.* New York, Macmillan, 1935.

Cannon, Carl L. *American Book Collectors and Collecting: From Colonial
Times to the Present.* New York, H. W. Wilson, 1941.

Friedlander, Janet. "Setting up a Special Collection on Water Pollution in a
University Library." *Special Libraries* 65:291-96 (July 1974).

Matheson, William. "An Approach to Special Collections." *American Libraries*
2:1150-56 (December 1971).
How Washington University built its manuscript collection of
contemporary American poets.

Metzdorf, Robert F. "Manuscript Collecting for Historical Societies."
Connecticut League of Historical Societies Bulletin 8:7-10 (Spring
1956).

Miller, Shirley. *The Vertical File and Its Satellites: A Handbook of Acquisition, Processing and Organization.* Littleton, Colo., Libraries Unlimited,
1971.
Contains imaginative suggestions on local materials to solicit and
possible donors.

Rush, Nixon Orwin. *Special Collections; What They Mean to Librarians,
Professors, and Collectors.* Tallahassee, Strozier Library, Friends
of the Florida State University, 1972.
How two special collections were collected, promoted, and used.

Sealock, Richard B. "Acquisition and Organization of Local History Materials
in Libraries." *Library Trends* 13:179-91 (October 1964).

CHAPTER 3
MATERIALS TO SOLICIT

Dupree, A. Hunter. "What Manuscripts the Historian Wants Saved." *Isis*
53:62-66 (March 1962).

Easterwood, Thomas Jefferson. "The Collecting and Care of Modern Manuscripts." *Call Number* (University of Oregon Library) 24, no. 1: 4-17
(Fall 1964).

Hill, Robert W. "Literary, Artistic and Musical Manuscripts." *Library Trends*
5:322-29 (January 1957).

McNeil, Donald R. "The Wisconsin Experiment." In: Wisconsin. State
Historical Society. *The American Collector.* Madison, The Society,
1955. pp. 33-44.

CHAPTER 4
SOURCES OF DONATIONS—LEADS

Altick, Richard D. *The Scholar Adventurers.* New York, Macmillan, 1950.
The most entertaining book on literary detection; the librarian
with imagination should be inspired to seek leads upon reading
this book.

Altrocchi, Rudolph. *Sleuthing in the Stacks.* Cambridge, Mass., Harvard University Press, 1944.

Benjamin, Mary A. *Autographs: A Key to Collecting.* 2nd ed., rev. New York, Walter R. Benjamin Autographs, 1963.

Burke, William Jeremiah. *American Authors and Books, 1640-1940.* New York, Gramercy Publishing, 1943.

Contemporary Authors: The International Bio-bibliographical Guide to Current Authors and Their Works, v.1- . Detroit, Gale Research, 1962-

Kunitz, Stanley Jasspon. *The Junior Book of Authors.* . . . New York, H. W. Wilson, 1934. Also: 2nd ed., New York, H. W. Wilson, 1951.

Kunitz, Stanley Jasspon. *Twentieth Century Authors: A Biographical Dictionary of Modern Literature.* New York, H. W. Wilson, 1942.

The National Cyclopaedia of American Biography. New York, J. T. White, 1893- .

The New York Times Index: A Master-Key to All Newspapers. New York, *The New York Times*, 1851- .

The New York Times Obituaries Index 1858-1968. New York, *The New York Times*, 1970.

Wakeman, John. *World Authors, 1950-1970: A Companion to Twentieth Century Authors.* New York, H. W. Wilson, 1975.

Wilson, H. W., firm, publishers. *Biography Index: A Cumulative Index to Biographical Materials in Books and Magazines*, v.1- . New York, author, 1946- .

Who's Who in America: A Biographical Dictionary of Notable Living Men and Women, v.1- . Chicago, A. N. Marquis, 1899- .

CHAPTER 5
CORRESPONDENCE

Kaiser, Barbara J. "Problems with Donors of Contemporary Collections." *American Archivist* 32:103-107 (April 1969).

CHAPTER 6
VISITING THE DONOR

Everitt, Charles P. *Adventures of a Treasure Hunter: A Rare Bookman in Search of American History.* Boston, Little, Brown, 1951.

Skiff, Frederick Woodward. *Adventures in Americana; Recollections of Forty Years Collecting Books, Furniture, China, Guns and Glass.* Portland, Oregon, Metropolitan Press, 1935.
The Everitt and Skiff autobiographies contrast sharply with the polished accounts by Randall, Powell, and Thompson. Everitt and Skiff recount with candor their experiences as bookmen, cajoling reluctant owners to sell books and manuscripts.

CHAPTER 7
RECEIPT, SORTING, ORGANIZATION,
DESCRIPTION, AND FINANCIAL APPRAISAL

American Library Association. Association of College and Research Libraries. Committee of the Rare Books and Manuscripts Section. Manuscripts Committee. "Statement on Appraisal of Gifts and on Legal Title." *American Libraries* 4:38 (January 1973).*
The policy is again being revised, but will probably recur indicating that the donor is financially responsible for appraisal of his gift.

American Library Association. Association of College and Research Libraries. Rare Books and Manuscripts Committee. "Universal Gift Forms and Instructions." *College and Research Libraries News,* no. 3:95-96 (March 1975).*

Archer, H. Richard. "Special Collections." *Library Trends* 18:354-62 (January 1970).

Briggs, Donald R. "Gift Appraisal Policy in Large Research Libraries." *College and Research Libraries* 29:505-507 (November 1968).

---

*In Spring 1977, the Association of College and Research Libraries gathered these two titles into one pamphlet, "Guidelines on Manuscripts and Archives" (Chicago 1977). The guidelines include statements on appraisals of gifts, legal title, access to original materials, reproduction of manuscripts for non-commercial and commercial purposes, and universal gift form and instructions. The pamphlet is free.

Brubaker, Robert L. "Archival Principles and the Creator of Manuscripts." *American Archivist* 29:505-514 (October 1966).

Burnette, Lawrence O., Jr. *Beneath the Footnote: A Guide to the Use and Preservation of American Historical Resources.* Madison, State Historical Society of Wisconsin, 1969.

Duckett, Kenneth. *Modern Manuscripts.*
Cited also in Chapter 1, this text is the most comprehensive in the field, with full statement of theory and then practical application.

Finch, Herbert. "Gifts, Appraisals and Taxes." *Cornell University Libraries Bulletin* 189:7-10 (May 1974).

Hodson, John Howard. *The Administration of Archives.* Oxford, Pergamon Press, 1972.

Kane, Lucile M. *A Guide to the Care and Administration of Manuscripts.* 2nd ed. Nashville, American Association for State and Local Historians, 1966.
Duckett's book, cited in Chapter 1, has taken the place of this long-respected volume.

Lytle, Richard H., ed. *Management of Archives and Manuscript Collections for Librarians.*
Cited in Chapter 1.

Schellenberg, Theodore R. *The Management of Archives.* New York, Columbia University Press, 1965.

"Writings on Archives, Historical Manuscripts, and Current Records." *American Archivist* 37:435-57 (July 1974); 38:339-74 (July 1975). Annual bibliography.

CHAPTER 8
MAINTAINING DONOR INTEREST

Basler, Roy P. "The Modern Collector." In: Wisconsin. State Historical Society. *The American Collector.* Madison, The Society, 1955. pp. 24-35.

Blosser, S. S. *Southern Historical Collection: A Guide to Manuscripts.* Chapel Hill, University of North Carolina, 1970.

Duniway, David C. "Conflict in Collecting." *American Archivist* 24:55-63 (January 1961).

Maryland Historical Society. *Manuscript Collection of the Maryland Historical Society*. Baltimore, The Society, 1968.

Oregon. University. Library. *Catalogue of Manuscripts in the University of Oregon Library*. Compiled by Martin Schmitt. Eugene, Oregon, University of Oregon, 1971.

CHAPTER 12
PROFESSIONAL AND PERSONAL QUALITIES

Krasean, Thomas K. "Impressions of a Field Representative in Search of Historical Manuscripts." *Library Occurrent* 23:123-24 (November 1969).

SUBJECT INDEX

Address books, 27
Antiquarian Booksellers Association of
  America, 113
Appraisals, 66-67, 79
Autographs, 26-27

Blanket solicitation
  See Leads, blanket solicitation
Book collections, 55
  alternatives to acceptance of, 113-14
  binding, 111-12
  case study of economics textbook, 112-13
  historical evaluation of, 105-106
  immediate valuation of, 106
  physical condition of, 107
  policy statement regarding, 114
  selection from, 109-110
  terms of gift, 107-108
Book collectors, 108-109
Book dealers
  See Leads, bookdealers as, 40-41
Business records, 29

Children's literature
  See "Golden age" of children's literature
  collection
Collection growth, 15-17, 22-23
Collection materials, 24-25
Community evaluation
  See Planning, community evaluation
Competition among libraries, 74
Cooperation among libraries, 73-75, 92
  microfilming, 74
  photocopying, 74
Corporate records, 29
Correspondence, 25-26

Correspondence with donor, 43, 81-82, 100
  continuing contact, 68-69, 104
  files, 47, 71-73
  first letter, 43-45
  follow-up letter, 46
  inventory transmittal, 64-65
  See also Deed of gift

Dead card files, 72
Deed of gift, 59-60
Diaries, 25
Discard, 65-66
Donor
  See Correspondence with donor; Leads,
  donors as; Visit with donor

Financial support
  See Planning, financial support

Geographical card files, 71-72
"Golden age" of children's literature
  collection, 76-88

Inventory
  See Receipt of gift, inventory

Journals, 25

Leads, associates and friends as, 38-39
  blanket solicitation, 41-42
  book dealers as, 40-41
  city directories, 35-36
  clipping files, 37
  collectors as, 41

Leads (cont'd)
  donors as, 39-40, 84
  evaluation of, 94-95
  in case study, 80-81
  library sources, 33-34, 38
  manuscript collections, 38
  mug books, 37
  newspaper files and indices, 36-37
  professional sources, 34-35
  records of, 94
  telephone directories, 35
Letters
  See Correspondence
Library collection evaluation
  See Planning, library collection
  evaluation
Local history, business, 20-22
  case study of music solicitation program,
    89-104
  collection growth, 22-23
  cultural, 19
  environmental, 19-20
  personal, 22
  professional, 20
  social, 19, 22

Magazines, 32
Manufacturers' catalogs, 29
Manuscripts, definition of, 25
Membership files, 28
Microfilming
  See Cooperation among libraries,
  microfilming
Miscellany, 32
Mug books, 37, 92, 112
Music solicitation program, 89-104

Name card files, 71
National collections, 23
  case study of "Golden age" of children's
  literature, 76-88

Oral history, 31

Pamphlets, 31
Photocopying
  See Cooperation among libraries,
  photocopying
Photographs, 30

Planning, aims of, 11
  community evaluation, 13, 77, 89-90
  financial support, 13, 78
  information resources, 91-92
  library collection evaluation, 12, 76-77,
    91-92
  user evaluation, 12, 77, 90-91
Press releases, 70, 88
Printing, 31
Public relations, 70

Receipt of gift, 58-59, 102
  inventory, 64-65, 85-88
  physical receipt, 60
  records, 60

Scope, 14-15
  of "Golden age" of children's literature
    collection, 76-77, 79-80
  of local history collection, 18
  of music solicitation program, 92-94
Scrapbooks, 28
Shipment of materials, 54
Solicitation program evaluation, direct
    benefits, 123-24
  future benefits, 124-25
  immediate benefits, 125
Solicitor, decision-making ability, 119-20
  institutional role, 116-17
  integrity of, 121
  personal qualities, 120-21
  professional qualities, 117-18
Sorting and arrangement, 61-62, 84-85,
    102-103
  techniques, 62-63
Sorting and packing, 52-54, 83
Special records, 29
Speeches, 27
Staffing, 13

Tax Reform Act of 1969, 67, 79

User evaluation
  See Planning, user evaluation

Visit with donor, 48, 82-83, 101-102
  appearance of solicitor, 48-49
  assessment of donor, 49-50, 101
  commitments, 55-56
  field notes, 56, 73
  general theories, 57
  personal reminiscence, 94-99
  return visit, 69-70
  solicitor's mistakes, 57
  solicitor's role, 50-52